Student's Workbook

# The New Episcopal Way

### A Course for the Classroom
### or
### Independent Study

by
CARL G. CARLOZZI, D. MIN.

MOREHOUSE PUBLISHING
Harrisburg, PA

**Morehouse Publishing**

*Editorial Office:*

871 Ethan Allen Highway
Ridgefield, CT 06877

*Corporate Office:*

P.O. Box 1321
Harrisburg, PA 17105

ISBN, Master Book: 0-8192-4102-4,
        Student's Workbook: 0-8192-4101-6

*Printed in the United States of America*
by
BSC LITHO
Harrisburg, PA

*To*
*Muriel S. McClellan, Ph.D.*
*my friend, lover,*
*wife, and golfing partner*

**Be a good evangelist. . . .**

**Invite and bring a friend to church.**

# Contents

In Appreciation . . . . . . . . . . . . . . . . . . . . . . . . . . . . . . . . . . . . . . . . . . . . . . 6

Introduction . . . . . . . . . . . . . . . . . . . . . . . . . . . . . . . . . . . . . . . . . . . . . . . . 7

Resource Directory and Bibliography . . . . . . . . . . . . . . . . . . . . . . . . . . 10

  1. Introduction to Theology . . . . . . . . . . . . . . . . . . . . . . . . . . . 15

  2. Bible Basics . . . . . . . . . . . . . . . . . . . . . . . . . . . . . . . . . . . . . . 21

  3. Our Christian Heritage . . . . . . . . . . . . . . . . . . . . . . . . . . . . . . 29

  4. Church Government and Canon Law . . . . . . . . . . . . . . . . . . . . . 37

  5. Prayer Book and Hymnal Usage . . . . . . . . . . . . . . . . . . . . . . . 49

  6. The Creeds: Historic Statements of Belief . . . . . . . . . . . . . . . . 59

  7. Moral and Ethical Living . . . . . . . . . . . . . . . . . . . . . . . . . . . . . 67

  8. The Personal Devotional Life . . . . . . . . . . . . . . . . . . . . . . . . . 75

  9. The Daily Office . . . . . . . . . . . . . . . . . . . . . . . . . . . . . . . . . . . 83

10. Church Customs and Symbolism . . . . . . . . . . . . . . . . . . . . . . 91

11. Sacraments and Ministry . . . . . . . . . . . . . . . . . . . . . . . . . . . . 99

12. Holy Baptism and Confirmation . . . . . . . . . . . . . . . . . . . . . . .107

13. The Holy Eucharist . . . . . . . . . . . . . . . . . . . . . . . . . . . . . . . .115

    Appendix: The Complete Prayer Book Subject and Topic Index . . .121

# In Appreciation

I wish to express special thanks to my staff at All Saints' who each assisted and endured the writing of this book in their own unique fashion; . . . and to my wardens, vestry, and parishioners, truly the most loving of parish families, who accorded me the study leave to write this book.

                                                                    C.G.C.

# Introduction

Welcome to the exciting opportunity of exploring the life and teachings of the Episcopal Church. We are a church that seeks to understand God's will and purpose for us in and through a grounding in Scripture, an appreciation for rational inquiry, and a respect for a continually evolving Christian tradition that bespeaks the power and renewing voice of the Holy Spirit in our midst.

This course of instruction, having both a "Master Book" and a "Student Workbook," has been designed to provide the following three options:

1. through the traditional use of a Master Book and Student Workbooks, to provide both a course instructor and his or her students with all the necessary materials needed for effective classroom teaching; and/or

2. through the exclusive use of the Master Book by both the course instructor *and* his or her students, to provide, with adult classes, the opportunity to use these materials in a seminar format of reading and discussion; and/or

3. through use of the Master Book alone, to provide interested persons with a self-taught course of independent study outside the classroom setting.

Accordingly, in this latter capacity, the Master Book has the potential of being an effective promotional and evangelical tool of practical benefit when it is made available to those who wish to answer the question, "The Episcopal Church: What's it all about?"

My predecessor in this parish, the late Fr. Paul D. Urbano, was fond of saying, "The Church exists for those who do not yet belong to it." These sentiments mark well our commission from Christ to preach the gospel, share the faith, care for the poor and dispossessed, and keep always in mind Jesus' teaching in the parable of the laborers in the vineyard (Matt. 20:1-16). And then, once having welcomed into our Christian household a new member, we and they are exhorted by St. Paul to "grow in the grace and knowledge of our Lord and Savior Jesus Christ" (2 Peter 3:18).

Therefore, since growth implies "movement" and knowledge is a "road to be traveled" as opposed to a destination, our mandate from Christ calls us continually to read again the great message of Scripture and to investigate and search out its meaning for our life today.

It is my sincere prayer that you may come to see and appreciate the benefits of the Episcopal difference.

The Reverend Carl G. Carlozzi, D. Min.
Rector, All Saints' Church and Day School
Phoenix, Arizona
Lent, 1992

# How To Use This Book
## as A Course Instructor

This course of instruction uses as its reading base for background information and lecture preparation the seven-volume "Church's Teaching Series," M.J. Hatchett's *Commentary on the American Prayer Book,* W.E. Post's *Saints, Signs and Symbols,* and the *Oxford Dictionary of the Christian Church.* All of these books are readily available for purchase, as you will note in the "Resource Directory and Bibliography." Further, all of these books are found in most parish libraries.

The Master Book of this course follows in exact detail the Student's Workbook with the following exceptions: the Master Book contains a full resource directory and bibliography; selected background reading and general reference suggestions; notes on ways to begin each class session and/or things to do to stimulate interest and involvement; suggestions on points to be highlighted in your lectures; optional class handout materials; visual aid information; and, of course, all the answers. In short, every effort has been made to assist you in presenting an edifying course of instruction that you can use either as is or adapt and enhance according to your own style and interests.

Here are some suggestions of a practical nature:
1. All class members should be given a Student Workbook, which is theirs to keep.
2. Pacing the class according to interest and the flow of discussion enhances learning.
3. An examination at the end of the course will serve as a stimulus for attendance, as well as provide an opportunity to integrate learning.
4. Providing time before each class session for special questions and concerns is most beneficial.
5. Use of the Master Book, instead of the Student Workbook, by those who cannot attend class but who wish to do independent study, will prove to be practical and most beneficial.

## Special Note
## To Those Teaching Adult Classes

Some course instructors will find, according to their style of teaching, especially with adult classes, that exclusive use of the Master Book, as opposed to the Student Workbook, by all class members provides an atmosphere more conducive to a lecture, question, and discussion format. If this is done, all class members should be instructed to read, prior to the beginning of each new topic, all "Background Reading" and "General Reference" suggestions listed in the "Preparation Suggestions for the Course Instructor." This will provide the potential for a more informed and lively class discussion but will also demand more of the instructor in terms of his or her own preparation. In short, openness and flexibility are the key ingredients in designing a course that best fits the needs and abilities of the students, as well as the preferred teaching style of the instructor.

## How To Use This Book
## for Independent Study

This course of instruction uses as its background reading base material taken from the seven-volume "Church's Teaching Series," M.J. Hatchett's *Commentary on the American Prayer Book,* W.E. Post's *Saints, Signs and Symbols,* and the *Oxford Dictionary of the Christian Church.* All of these books are readily available for purchase, as you will note in the "Resource Directory and Bibliography." Further, all of these books are found in most parish libraries.

In making the most effective use of this book for independent study, consider yourself your own "course instructor." Accordingly, the following orderly suggestions will prove helpful:

1. After consulting the "Preparation Suggestions for the Course Instructor" at the beginning of the chapter being studied, read all the materials suggested under the headings of "Background Reading" and "General Reference."
2. Study the material presented in the text of each chapter in light of your reading and, where indicated, look up the Prayer Book cross-references.
3. Quiz yourself by looking at the teaching goals listed under "Basic Information to Be Highlighted in Lecture" and, if you feel there are deficiencies in your understanding, expand the scope of your reading beyond the initial suggestions presented.

In summary, should you find at the end of your study that you need clarification on any matter, I encourage you to make an appointment with your priest.

# Resource Directory and Bibliography of Books and Materials Referred to in This Course

## Course Background Reading

*The Church's Teaching Series*

U.T. Holmes III, J.H. Westerhoff III, *Christian Believing* (Seabury Press, 1979). Distributed by Harper & Row.

R.A. Bennett, and O.C. Edwards, *The Bible for Today's Church* (Seabury Press, 1979). Distributed by Harper & Row.

J.E. Booty, *The Church in History* (Seabury Press, 1979). Distributed by Harper & Row.

R.A. Norris, *Understanding the Faith of the Church* (Seabury Press, 1979). Distributed by Harper & Row.

C.P. Price, and L. Weil, *Liturgy for Living* (Seabury Press, 1979). Distributed by Harper & Row.

E.H. Brill, *The Christian Moral Vision* (Seabury Press, 1979). Distributed by Harper & Row.

R. Hosmer, A. Jones and J.H. Westerhoff III, *Living in the Spirit* (Seabury Press, 1979). Distributed by Harper & Row.

*Other*

M.J. Hatchett, *Commentary on the American Prayer Book* (Seabury Press, 1980). Distributed by Harper & Row.

W.E. Post, *Saints, Signs and Symbols* (Harrisburg, PA: Morehouse Publishing, 1974).

NOTE: Harper & Row's toll free "book order number" is 1-800-328-5125. Morehouse Publishing's order number is 1-800-877-0012.

## General Reference Materials

**The Church Hymnal Corporation,** 800 Second Avenue, New York, NY 10017; (212) 661-6700. Prayer books, hymnals, specialty titles on liturgy, church music, and Episcopal Church related subjects. Catalog on request. Source for the following:

    C.G. Carlozzi, ed., *Prayers for Pastor and People*

    R. Glover, ed., *The Hymnal (1982) Companion*

    D. Schmidt, *Hymnal Studies Seven*

    M. Hatchett, *Hymnal Studies Eight*

**Oxford University Press,** 200 Madison Avenue, New York, NY 10016; 1-800-451-7556. Catalog on request. Source for the following:

    F.L. Cross, ed., *The Oxford Dictionary of the Christian Church*

**Morehouse Publishing,** P.O. Box 1321, Harrisburg, PA 17105; 1-800-877-0012. Christian education (books, resource materials, audio-visuals) and general religious titles of practical benefit. Catalog on request. Source for the following:

    E.A. Kelley, ed., *The Episcopal Church Annual*

## Class Handout Material Suppliers

**Forward Movement Publications,** 412 Sycamore Street, Cincinnati, OH 45202-4195; (513) 721-6659 and (800) 543-1813. Very large tract selection on every aspect of church life. Catalog on request. Recommendations listed at the beginning of each chapter in "Preparation Suggestions for the Course Instructor."

**Channing L. Bete Co.,** 200 State Road, South Deerfield, MA 01373; (413) 665-7611 and (800) 628-7733. Short, illustrated minibooklets on a host of practical religious and secular topics. Catalog on request. Recommendations listed at the beginning of each chapter in "Preparation Suggestions for the Course Instructor."

**Morehouse Publishing,** P.O. Box 1321, Harrisburg, PA 17105; 1-800-877-0012. Christian education (books, resource materials, audio-visuals) and general religious titles of practical benefit. Catalog on request. A good source to do some browsing on your own for special items. Recommendations listed at the beginning of each chapter in "Preparation Suggestions for the Course Instructor."

## Visual Aid Suppliers

**Episcopal Radio-TV Foundation,** 3379 Peachtree Road N.E., Atlanta, GA 30326. Order from Morehouse Publishing as noted above. Superb video cassette presentations on religious topics of interest to Episcopalians. Audio cassettes on many subjects also available. Catalog and "updated" mailers available from Morehouse Publishing on request. Selection of materials is left to the discretion of the course instructor.

**EcuFilm,** 810 Twelfth Avenue South, Nashville, TN 37203; (615) 242-6277 and (800) 251-4091. Consolidated film and video resources maintained by seven denominations (including Episcopal) plus National Council and World Council of Churches. Wide selection on a multitude of subjects. Catalog on request. Selection of materials is left to the discretion of the course instructor.

# NOTES

# NOTES

# NOTES

# 1. Introduction to Theology

1. The Gospel of St. John sets forth one of the most basic statements of the Christian faith when it notes,

   For God so _____ the world, that

   he _____ his only begotten Son, that

   _____ believeth in him should

   not _____, but have everlasting

   _____. (John 3:16)

   The adventure of asking questions about who this God is, what his purposes are, and how he has accomplished and continues to accomplish these purposes in

   the world is known as the study of _____.


2. In the Anglican tradition (that worldwide fellowship of churches having their roots in and communion with the Church of England), our theological inquiry has always been grounded in the following threefold source of authority dating back to the works of Anglican divine Richard Hooker and other earlier theologians:

   a. _____

   b. _____

   c. _____


3. The Anglican theological contention, having its grounding in what has often been called the "three-leg stool" of Scripture, reason, and tradition, is that one will only arrive at a proper understanding of God when theological pursuit is based upon:

   a. the Bible as an inspired but not

   _____

   product of the community of faith, reflecting the culture and scientific understanding of the time;

   b. the openness of free, rational inquiry as opposed to _____ faith; and

   c. the tradition of an _____

   _____ that hears and follows the lead of the Holy Spirit in each new generation.

4. The God whom we seek to know and understand is "one God" who has revealed himself to us in three ways. These three avenues of self-disclosure are known theologically as:

   a. _____ = God's revelation of himself, outside of the Bible, through nature, Creation, and the moral consciousness of humanity.

   b. _____ = History of Israel, both old and new, especially and uniquely in the person of Jesus Christ.

   c. _____ = Presence of the Holy Spirit within the ongoing life of the Christian Church.

5. The God whom we seek to know and understand is "one God" who has carried out his relationship with us in three distinct ways, in the same way that you are "one individual" who may be known as a father (or mother) in one relationship, a spouse in another relationship, and an uncle (or aunt) in yet another relationship. Accordingly, the "one God" we worship has related himself to the human family in a three-fold fashion known theologically as the "three persons" of the

   _____.

   a. First, God relates himself to us as the "unseen" _____ of the Old Testament.

   b. Second, God relates himself to us as the "visible" _____ of the New Testament.

   c. Third, God relates himself to us as the "inwardly felt" _____ of the Continuing Testament known as the Church.

6. The Church, as the Continuing Testament of believers empowered by the Holy Spirit, lives out and fulfills what the Old and New Testament can only relate to

   us in _____; for while we understand the Bible to be

   the Word of God, we do not believe it to be _____ that God has ever spoken or will ever speak.

7. Living and walking "in the Spirit" and relying on the Old and New Testament as our road map and guide, we, the Church, as the living Body of Christ, go forth

   into life seeking to hear and discover and understand God's _____

   _____, as revealed by the _____ in each new day and generation in and through our personal, corporate, and liturgical lives.

8. In 1 Cor. 12:13-27 (please read the passage), St. Paul draws the metaphor of the

Church being _____.
This diversity reminds us that God speaks to us in many different ways that are all

_____ and that he calls us to very different ministries that are

all _____. Accordingly, when we see the multitude of denomi-
national ministries, we are called by God to remember that we are all branch

offices of the _____ and that God's work is crippled

when one branch office begins to think and act as if it were the _____

_____.

9. When we break God's commandments or fall away from the teachings of Jesus

Christ we commit what is known as _____, a term that the
Book of Common Prayer (p. 848) defines as "the seeking of our own will instead
of the will of God, thus distorting our relationship with God, with ourselves, with
other people, and with all creation." The word *sin* has its roots in an old archery

term that means _____. And as St. Paul reminds us,

_____, from time to time, falls short of the glory of God and
"misses the mark."

10. Theologically and practically it is important to remember that God _____

sin but _____ the sinner. Accordingly, when we sin, God gives

us out of his love an _____ "to turn our lives around" known

as _____, a term that comes from the Greek word *metanoia.*
Therefore, a sinner is someone who recognizes that he or she has "missed the
mark" in their relationships with God and humanity and then, quite happily, is

given the chance to _____ with a clear conscience as
a "forgiven" child of God.

11. Just as human beings often miss the mark in their relationships, _____
itself often misses the mark in terms of the bad or evil things that happen to

people. When the Bible notes that rain falls "on the _____

and on the _____" (Matt. 5:45), it reminds us, that God does

not _____ anyone from life's painful realities with magic
spiritual umbrellas. Instead, God provides the believer with an inward spiritual
power to "triumph over every evil" and to say confidently with St. Paul in Rom.
8:38-39:

For I am sure that neither death, nor life, nor angels, nor principalities, nor things present, nor things to come, nor powers, nor height, nor depth, nor

_____, will be able to separate us from the love of God in Christ Jesus our Lord.

Theologically, then, the Christian's "difference that makes the difference" is

the ability to _____ pain and evil instead of avoiding it or

being _____ by it.

12. When we speak of "eternal life" we are talking about being in an _____

_____ with God, for as Jesus put it in John 17:3, "And this is eternal life, that they know thee the only true God, and Jesus Christ whom thou hast sent." The theological term that refers to the fulfillment of our ongoing relationship with God following physical death, and prior to the Second Coming

of Christ, is known as _____. That same state of ongoing relationship with God, following both physical death and the Second Coming

of Christ, is known as _____. Accordingly, "heaven" is the state of existence in which God's love encompasses everything.

13. The state of existence in which God's love is willfully forsaken by us or perceived to be absent by us, both in this life and after physical death, is known as

_____. The Bible reminds us, however, that God's love continues to be offered to those who are in hell, as is made manifest by St. Paul's

observation that "Jesus came into the world to _____"
(1 Tim. 1:15) and by St. Peter's observation that Jesus also "went and preached

to the spirits in _____" (this being the apostle's language in 1 Pet. 3:19 for those locked into an existence apart from God's love after their physical death).

# NOTES

# NOTES

## 2. Bible Basics

1. It is the universally held position of the Anglican communion that the Holy

   Scriptures of the Old and New Testaments contain _____

   _____; and indeed, all persons to be ordained as deacons,

   priests, or bishops must make this assent as part of their _____

   _____ (see the Book of Common Prayer [B.C.P.], pp. 513, 526,
   and 538). Three of the most basic beliefs "necessary to salvation" and based
   in the Holy Scriptures are the following:

   a. The personal acceptance of _____.

   b. Belief that Christ _____ from the dead.

   c. The willingness to _____ your sins, accept God's for-

      giveness, and then to _____ as you have been forgiven.
   What other things can you think of that are "necessary to salvation" according
   to the Bible?

2. While the Holy Scriptures contain all things necessary to salvation, it is the
   position of our church that the Holy Scriptures also contain some things

   _____ to salvation, such as,

   a. The _____ of the Genesis story of Creation.

   b. The _____ of scripture.

   c. The necessity of adhering to the _____ set forth in the
      Old Testament.
   d. The belief that the Second Coming will happen as described in the Book of

   _____.

   Are there other things that you can think of "unnecessary to salvation" set forth
   in the Bible?

3. The English word *bible,* which is derived from the Greek word _____,

   means, literally, _____. Later Greek usage rendered the

   meaning as _____ or venerable book. Why do we refer to

   the Bible as holy? _____

   _____

   _____

4. The Bible is divided into two distinct parts. These are known as the _____

_____ and _____. What does the word

*testament* mean or signify? _____

5. What is the nature and purpose of these two testaments, and between whom were they made?

a. _____

_____

_____

_____

b. _____

_____

_____

6. The Old Testament books, written originally in _____
(with the exception of Daniel, which was written in Greek), were composed over

a period of some one thousand years between the dates _____

and _____. The thirty-nine books of the Old Testament may
be divided into three significant sections or classifications. These are the
following:

a. _____

b. _____

c. _____

7. The Psalms, generally attributed to the writings of _____,
constitute some of the most beautiful religious poetic verse to be found in the
Bible and, in terms of subject matter, span the whole relationship between

_____ and _____. The Book of Common
Prayer, on pages 585-808, divides all one hundred and fifty psalms into an orderly
monthly pattern for reading each morning and evening.

8. In the Old Testament, God's desire and ability to make himself known to us,

called _____, takes place in and through three basic ways.
What are these three means of revelation, giving an example from the Bible of
each?

a. _____

_____

b. _____

_____

_____

c. _____

_____

_____

9. In coming to know God through these various means of revelation, the Old Testament builds to a prophetic climax in the Jews looking forward to the coming

of the _____. What does this Hebrew word mean? _____

_____

10. Where in the Old Testament will you find some of the most significant prophecies relating to the coming of the Messiah, his role in history, and his lot in life?

a. _____          d. _____

b. _____          e. _____

c. _____

11. The uniqueness of the New Testament is that God chose to make himself known in human form in the person of Jesus. This act of God's becoming man is known

as the _____. What does the Gospel of St. John have to say about this great mystery and act of God (see John 1:14, 16)?

And the _____ was made _____
and dwelt among us, and we beheld his glory,
the glory as of the only begotten of the

_____, full of grace and truth. . . .

And of his _____ have all we
received grace for grace.

12. The New Testament books, originally written in _____,
were composed at different times over a period of some fifty-four years between

_____ and _____.

The New Testament, consisting of _____ books, may be divided into the following four significant parts:

a. _____     c. _____

b. _____     d. _____

13. The word *gospel* means the _____ of God as proclaimed by his Son Jesus Christ. By which great evangelists were the Gospels written?

a. _____     c. _____

b. _____     d. _____

14. What are the nine most significant aspects of our Lord's life with which the Gospels deal?

a. _____     f. _____

b. _____     g. _____

c. _____     h. _____

d. _____     i. _____

e. _____

15. What story does the book titled "Acts of the Apostles," written by St. Luke, tell?

_____

_____

16. The word *epistle* means a _____. To whom, in general, were

the New Testament Epistles written? _____

_____

_____

17. The most well known and prolific writer of epistles is the Apostle St. _____. By whom were some of the other epistles written?

a. _____     c. _____

b. _____     d. _____

18. What are the four basic purposes of the New Testament Epistles?

a. _____

b. _____

c. _____

d. _____

19. The Book of Revelation, written by St. John, is a record of visions and prophetic

writings known as an _____.

What does this term mean? _____

_____

_____

_____

20. The central and most important belief proclaimed in the New Testament is that
of the Resurrection. What does this mean?

_____

_____

_____

_____

_____

21. Some Bibles include, between the Old Testament and the New Testament, a
section containing fourteen other books. What are these books called?

_____

# NOTES

# NOTES

# NOTES

# 3. Our Christian Heritage

1. The followers of our Lord Jesus received their initial command and commission to minister when Jesus said to them, in Matt. 28:19-20,

   Go therefore and make _____ of

   all nations, _____ them in the
   name of the Father and of the Son and of the
   Holy Spirit, teaching them to observe all that
   I have commanded you; and lo, I am with you

   _____, to the close of the age.

2. The fulfillment of Jesus' promise to be with his followers "always" came on that day when the disciples were empowered from on high by the gift of the

   _____. This day, often referred to as the Birthday of the

   Church, is known as _____.

3. The Fourth Commandment reminds us that we should keep holy the Sabbath day. If you were a good Jew and followed the Jewish Law, as did Jesus himself, which

   day of the week would you observe as the Sabbath? _____

4. Following the Crucifixion, the followers of Jesus stopped observing the Jewish Sabbath day as their principal day of worship. Instead, they began to observe

   _____ as the most fitting day in which to give thanks to God for all that he had done for humankind. Why was this change made?

   _____

   _____

   _____

5. In services of worship, or liturgies, on Sunday mornings, the early Christians always commemorated the joyful Resurrection of Christ by receiving and partaking

   of _____ and _____, which were blessed

   (or given thanks over) just as Jesus himself did at _____.

   The early Christians called this service the _____, a word of

   Greek derivation meaning _____.

6. Following all of the prayers the officiant said in the service, the early Christians responded, as we do today in our own worship, with the Hebrew word *Amen,*

   which means _____ or _____.

7. The early Christians had no hymnal or prayer book, as we do today, and in their

   services chanted and sang _____. The officiant, on the other

   hand, had to _____ prayers according to his or her own ability and the needs of the occasion. However, after the year A.D. 313—the year the

   Roman emperor _____ gave Christianity official status in the empire—forms of service began to be written down and standardized in all parts of the empire because services no longer had to be held in secret because of fear of persecution, the first major persecution being started under the Roman

   emperor _____ in A.D. 64.

8. The bulk of the dramatic spread of Christianity from Jerusalem to Asia Minor to Rome was accomplished through the missionary journeys and preaching of

   the Apostle St. _____, who in contrast to St. Peter, saw the necessity and appropriateness of taking the gospel beyond the Jewish community

   and preaching to the _____.

9. From A.D. 313 until the sixteenth century, and what historians call the

   _____, all of Christianity in Western Europe was under the control of Rome and the pope, that is, there were no denominations. There was

   just "one" church. In the East, however, there was the _____

   _____, which had separated from Rome about the year

   _____, denying papal authority but retaining the fullness of the Catholic faith.

Thomas Cranmer, Archbishop of Canterbury

30

10. In the year 1534, in the reign of English King _____,
the Catholic church in England severed its allegiance with the pope. The Church
of England, as it has since come to be known and from which our Episcopal
Church is descended, has remained faithful to the _____
tradition and to the _____ faith.

11. Following the break with Rome, the Church of England set out on a policy of
much-needed reform. In the year _____ the first Book of
Common Prayer was published under Archbishop of Canterbury _____
_____, who was the man most responsible for its issue and
content.

Title Page, *The Book of Common Prayer,*
1549

12. Name four objects of reform that the first Book of Common Prayer sought to achieve.

    a. _____

    b. _____

    c. _____

    d. _____

13. The Church of England had its beginning in America with the colonization of

    _____. It was here, in 1607, that the Reverend

    _____ celebrated the first service of Holy Communion. In this regard, Fr. Hunt noted in his journal, "We did hang an awning (which is an old sail) to three or four trees, til we cut planks, our pulpit a bar of wood nailed to two neighboring trees. This was our church till we built a homely thing like a barn, set upon crotchets covered with rafts, sedge, and earth. . . . Yet we had daily Common Prayer morning and evening, every Sunday two sermons, and every three months the Holy Communion" (J.T. Addison, *The Episcopal Church in the United States,* [New York: Charles Scribner's Sons, 1951], p. 28.)

Samuel Seabury

14. The American Episcopate had its beginning when, in 1784, the Reverend

_____ of Connecticut was consecrated as the first

Episcopal bishop in the United States by bishops of the _____

_____. The Reverend Mr. Seabury first endeavored
to be consecrated by bishops of the Church of England, but this was not possible

because of existing English statutes that required _____

_____ to and acknowledgement of the supremacy of the

_____. In 1787, after the passage of an act of English Parlia-

ment, the Reverend _____ of Pennsylvania and the Reverend

_____ of New York were consecrated bishops for the United
States in Lambeth Palace Chapel by English bishops. Thus, an American Episcopate, capable of sustaining its own existence, was born.

15. The first General Convention of the Episcopal Church in the United States of

America was held in _____ on July 28, 1789.
What were the three major achievements of this convention?

  a. _____

  b. _____

  c. _____

16. The dates of the three previous American books of common prayer are _____;

_____; and _____. The Book of Common Prayer of _____, authorized
for use by the General Convention, endeavors to achieve, among other things,
the following new features:

  a. _____

  b. _____

  c. _____

  d. _____

  e. _____

17. The Episcopal Church in the United States, and her sister churches throughout
the worldwide Anglican communion, share a common theological and liturgical
tradition, as well as a spiritual fellowship. These elements of commonality find
their focus in a meeting in London of all Anglican bishops every ten years. This

meeting is known as the _____ and is presided over

by the _____. The current occupant of this office

is the Most Reverend and Rt. Hon. _____.

The 103rd Archbishop of Canterbury
The Most Reverend and Right Honorable George Carey

# HISTORICAL DESCENT OF THE AMERICAN PRAYER BOOK*

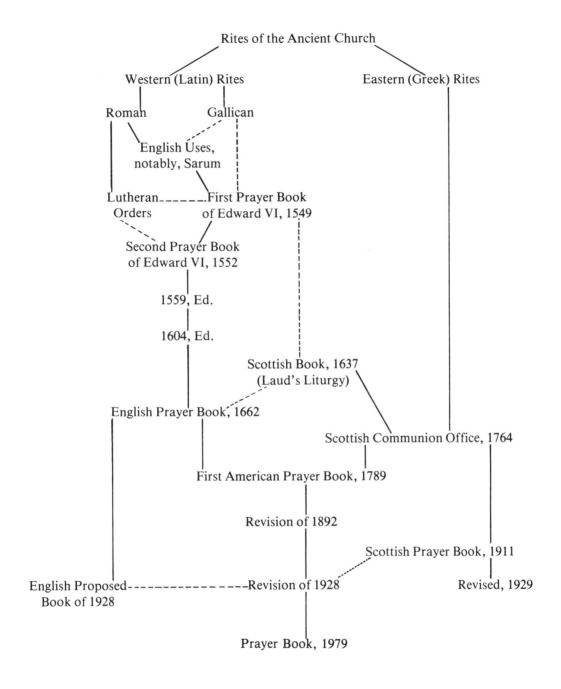

---

*M.H. Shepherd, Jr., *The Oxford American Prayer Book Commentary,* (New York: Oxford University Press, 1950, p. xxiii.). Used by permission.

# NOTES

# 4. Church Government and Canon Law

1. The Episcopal Church, nationally, has a legislative and policy-making body known

    as _____. This official governing body of our

    church meets every _____ years. The organizational structure
    of this governing body, like that of the United States Congress, is made up of
    two deliberating bodies or houses. They are:

    a. _____

    b. _____

House of Deputies in session at General Convention

2. While the House of Bishops is comprised solely of bishops, of whom is the House
    of Deputies composed?

    a. _____

    b. _____

3. Authorized by the General Convention is an administrative body whose function
    is to "have charge of the unification, development and prosecution of the
    Missionary, Educational, and Social Work of the Church, and of such other work
    as may be committed to it by the General Convention." What is the name and

    location of this administrative body? _____

    _____

4. The presiding bishop, ex officio the president of the Executive Council, is elected from the _____ by the House of Bishops, which election is then confirmed by the House of Deputies. What are four prime functions of the presiding bishop of our church in his or her role as the chief pastor? See Title I., Canon 2., Section 4 (a).

   a. _____

       _____

   b. _____

       _____

   c. _____

       _____

       _____

   d. _____

5. Our present presiding bishop is the Most Reverend _____,

the former diocesan bishop of _____.

6. Our national Episcopal Church is divided into numerous ecclesiastical/territorial units of administration and jurisdiction that are known as _____.

In which one of these do you live? _____.

7. The word *episcopal* comes from the Greek word _____,

which means _____.

8. Each diocese is presided over by a bishop who is referred to as the _____. Many dioceses have assistant bishops to help in the work of the church. An assistant bishop who is elected with the right of succession to the post of

diocesan is known as a _____. An assistant bishop

who is elected without the right of succession is known as a _____

_____. In those situations where the diocesan bishop does not call for an election but simply hires an "already consecrated bishop" to

assist, this bishop's title is that of _____.

Most Reverend Edmond L. Browning

```
                          Comparison Chart
    U.S. Government                        Episcopal Ch. Gov't
      President                              Presiding Bishop
      Congress                               General Convention
      (Senate)                               (House of Bishops)
      (House of Rep.)                        (House of Deputies)
      State                                  Diocese
      Governor                               Bishop
      Legislature                            Diocesan Convention
      City                                   Parish
      Mayor                                  Rector
      Council                                Vestry
```

9. Each diocese holds an annual _____ for the purposes of legislative and administrative policy, as well as for electing its own clerical and lay delegates to the _____.

10. On the local level, the Episcopal Church is comprised of ecclesiastical/territorial units of administration and pastoral responsibility known as _____ and _____. A mission is under the direct jurisdiction of the bishop, its minister being known as a _____; a parish is guided spiritually by a minister known as a _____.

11. The business and financial affairs of a parish are under the control of a _____, which is comprised of _____ who are elected by the parish at its own annual meeting. This annual meeting also elects lay-persons who, along with their rector, represent them at the _____ _____.

    (**NOTE:** A similar pattern is followed in missions under the bishop's supervision.)

12. The bishops of my diocese are:

    a. The Right Reverend _____
       (Diocesan)

    b. The Right Reverend _____
       (Coadjutor)

c. The Right Reverend _____
   (Suffragan)

d. The Right Reverend _____
   (Suffragan)

e. The Right Reverend _____
   (Assistant)

*Some Helpful Information
on Canon Law and Other Matters*

The Episcopal Church binds both clergy and laity by certain very specific regulations, laws, and directives that are laid down by both the national church and a particular diocese. Further, each parish and mission has its own constitution and bylaws that must be adhered to by the clergy and each parishioner.

In addition to many of the rubrics, directives, and regulations of canon law, about which you will learn in this course of study, the following is a list of regulations and directives, set forth by this church, of which you should be aware. At the end of the list you will find additional space that you may use to make appropriate notes relating to your own diocesan canons and parish or mission bylaws. Copies of the same, along with the constitution and canons of the Episcopal Church, may be obtained through consultation with your clergy.

Title I
**Canon 17.**
**Of Regulations Respecting the Laity**

Sec. 1 (a). All persons who have received the Sacrament of Holy Baptism with water in the Name of the Father, and of the Son, and of the Holy Spirit, whether in this Church or in another Christian Church, and whose Baptisms have been duly recorded in this Church, are members thereof.

(b). Members sixteen years of age and over are to be considered adult members.

(c). It is expected that all adult members of this Church, after appropriate instructions, will have made a mature public affirmation of their faith and commitment to the responsibilities of their Baptism and will have been confirmed or received by a Bishop of this Church or by a Bishop of a Church in communion with this Church.

Sec. 2 (a). All members of this Church who have received Holy Communion in this Church at least three times during the preceding year are to be considered communicants of this Church.

Sec. 3. All communicants of this Church who for the previous year have been faithful in corporate worship, unless for good cause prevented, and have been faithful in working, praying, and giving for the spread of the Kingdom of God, are to be considered communicants in good standing.

Sec. 4 (a). A member of this Church removing from the congregation in which his or her membership is recorded shall procure a certificate of membership indicating that he or she is recorded as a member (or adult member) of this Church and whether or not such a member:

1. is a communicant;
2. is recorded as being in good standing;
3. has been confirmed or received by a Bishop of this Church or a Bishop in communion with this Church.

Upon acknowledgment that a member who has received such a certificate has been enrolled in another congregation of this or another Church, the Minister or Warden issuing the certificate shall remove the name of the person from the parish register.

Sec. 5. No one shall be denied rights or status in this Church because of race, color, or ethnic origin.

Sec. 6. A person to whom the Sacraments of the Church shall have been refused, or who has been repelled from the Holy Communion under the rubrics, or who desires a judgment as to his or her status in the Church, may lodge a complaint or application with the Bishop or Ecclesiastical Authority. No Minister of this Church shall be required to admit to the Sacraments a person so refused or repelled without the written direction of the Bishop or Ecclesiastical Authority. The Bishop or Ecclesiastical Authority may in certain circumstances see fit to require the person to be admitted or restored because of the insufficiency of the cause assigned by the Minister. If it shall appear to the Bishop or Ecclesiastical Authority that there is sufficient cause to justify refusal of the Holy Communion, however, appropriate steps shall be taken to institute such inquiry as may be directed by the Canons of the Diocese; and should no such Canon exist, the Bishop or Ecclesiastical Authority shall proceed according to such principles of law and equity as will insure an impartial investigation and judgment.

Sec. 7. No unbaptized person shall be eligible to receive Holy Communion in this Church.


Title I
## Canon 18.
## Of the Solemnization of Holy Matrimony

Sec. 2. No Minister of this Church shall solemnize any marriage unless the following conditions are complied with:

(a). The Minister shall have ascertained the right of the parties to contract a marriage according to the laws of the State.

(b). The Minister shall have ascertained that both parties understand that Holy Matrimony is a physical and spiritual union of a man and a woman, entered into within the community of faith, by mutual consent of heart, mind, and will, and with intent that it be lifelong.

(c). The Minister shall have ascertained that both parties freely and knowingly consent to such marriage, without fraud, coercion, mistake as to the identity of a partner, or mental reservation.

(d). The Minister shall have ascertained that at least one of the parties has received Holy Baptism.

(e). The Minister shall have instructed both parties as to the nature, meaning, and purpose of Holy Matrimony, or have ascertained that they have both received such instruction from persons known by him or her to be competent and responsible.

Sec. 3. No Minister of this Church shall solemnize any marriage unless the following procedures are complied with:

(a). The intention of the parties to contract marriage shall have been signified to the Minister at least thirty days before the service of solemnization; "Provided," that for weighty cause, the Minister may dispense with this requirement, if one of the parties is a member of his or her Congregation, or can furnish satisfactory evidence of his or her responsibility. In case the thirty days notice is waived, the Minister shall report his action in writing to the Bishop immediately.

Sec. 4. It shall be within the discretion of any Minister of this Church to decline to solemnize any marriage.

Title I
**Canon 19.**
**Of Regulations Respecting the Holy Matrimony: Concerning Preservation of Marriage, Dissolution of Marriage, and Re-marriage**

Sec. 1. When marital unity is imperiled by dissension, it shall be the duty of either or both parties, before contemplating legal action, to lay the matter before a Minister of this Church; and it shall be the duty of such Minister to labor that the parties may be reconciled.

Sec. 2 (a). Any member of this Church whose marriage has been annulled or dissolved by a civil court may apply to the bishop or Ecclesiastical Authority of the Diocese in which such person is legally or canonically resident for a judgment as to his or her marital status in the eyes of the Church. Such judgment may be a recognition of the nullity, or of the termination of said marriage; "Provided," that no such judgment shall be construed as affecting in any way the legitimacy of children or the civil validity of the former relationship.

Sec. 3. No Minister of this Church shall solemnize the marriage of any person who has been the husband or wife of any other person then living, nor shall any member of this Church enter into a marriage when either of the contracting parties has been the husband or the wife of any other person then living, except as hereinafter provided:

(a). The Minister shall be satisified by appropriate evidence that the prior marriage has been annulled or dissolved by a final judgment or decree of a civil court of competent jurisdiction.

(b). The Minister shall have instructed the parties that continuing concern must be shown for the well-being of the former spouse and of any children of the prior marriage.

(c). The Minister shall consult with and obtain the consent of the Minister's Bishop prior to, and shall report to that Bishop, the solemnization of any marriage under this Section.

(d). If the proposed marriage is to be solemnized in a jurisdiction other than the one in which the consent has been given, the consent shall be affirmed by the Bishop of that jurisdiction.

Sec. 4. All provisions of Canon I. 18 shall, in all cases, apply.


## Other Matters of Interest

1. The control of the worship and the spiritual jurisdiction of the Parish are vested in the Rector, subject to the Rubrics of the Book of Common Prayer, the Canons of the Church, and the godly counsel of the Bishop (Title III., Canon 15., Sec. 1 (a).).
2. For the purposes of his or her office and for the full and free discharge of all functions and duties pertaining thereto, the Rector shall, at all times, be entitled to the use and control of the Church and Parish buildings with the appurtenances and furniture thereof (Title III., Canon 15., Sec. 1 (c).).
3. Except as provided by the law of the State or of the Diocese, the Vestry shall be agents and legal representatives of the Parish in all matters concerning its corporate property and the relations of the Parish to its Clergy (Title I., Canon 14., Sec. 2.).
4. The Book of Common Prayer as now established or hereafter amended by the authority of this Church, shall be in use in all the Dioceses (Constitution, first sentence of Article X).
5. The Minister of the Congregation is directed to instruct the people, from time to time, about the duty of Christian parents to make prudent provision for the well-being of their families, and of all persons to make wills, while they are in health, arranging for the disposal of their temporal goods, not neglecting, if they are able, to leave bequests for religious and charitable purposes (B.C.P., p. 445).
6. In case of illness, the Minister of the Congregation is to be notified (B.C.P., p. 453). If the sick person desires the Communion (whether at home, hospital, nursing home, etc.), it is desirable that fellow parishioners, relatives, and friends be present, when possible, to make their Communion with the sick person (B.C.P., p. 396). Further, if a person desires to receive the Sacrament, but, by reason of extreme sickness or physical disability, is unable to eat and drink the Bread and Wine, the Celebrant is to assure that person that all the benefits of Communion are received, even though the Sacrament is not received with the mouth (B.C.P., p. 457).
7. When a person is near death, the Minister of the Congregation should be notified, in order that the ministrations of the Church may be provided (B.C.P., p. 462).

8. The death of a member of the Church should be reported as soon as possible to, and arrangements for the funeral should be made in consultation with, the Minister of the Congregation. Baptized Christians are properly buried from the church, the service being held at a time when the congregation has an opportunity to be present, the coffin being closed before the service (B.C.P., p. 468). Further, it is appropriate that family and friends come together for prayers prior to the funeral (B.C.P., p. 465).

*Notes on Diocesan Canons and/or*
*Parish or Mission Bylaws*
*(Use space below)*

# NOTES

# NOTES

## 5. Prayer Book and Hymnal Usage

1. One of the glories of our Anglican heritage, for over four centuries, has been the majesty of the worship. The format for this worship has been set forth in a series of continuing editions of the Book of Common Prayer. Title II., Canon 3., Sec. 1.

   declares the copy of the edition of _____, as accepted by General Convention, to be "Standard Book of Common Prayer" and Article X. of the constitution declares that "The Book of Common Prayer as now established

   or hereafter amended by the authority of this Church _____

   in use in _____ the Dioceses."

2. The 1979 Book of Common Prayer, along with all previous editions from 1549

   through 1928, endeavors to set forth the Christian faith in one _____

   _____ for corporate and personal _____

   use by the people of God, _____ to the many and various situations and occasions of life. In a real sense, the Book of Common Prayer translates Scripture, reason, and tradition into a book of public and private worship.

3. In the conducting of and participation in the worship of the church, what is the

   purpose of rubrics and how can they be identified? _____

   _____

   _____

4. In addition to the rubrics, where are the three other specific places in the Book of Common Prayer in which you will find the necessary rules and directions relating to the overall rationale and use of the book?

   a. _____

   _____

   b. _____

   _____

   c. _____

   _____

5. Under what circumstances may any of the Proper Liturgies for Special Days, the Pastoral Offices, and the Episcopal Services be conformed to the traditional language from the contemporary idiom (see B.C.P., p. 14)? _____

_____

_____

6. What are the three regular services appointed for public worship in the Episcopal Church (see B.C.P., p. 13)?

    a. _____

    b. _____

    c. _____

7. Which of these three regular services is to be used as the principal act of public worship on all Sundays and major feasts (see B.C.P., p. 13)? _____

_____

8. Under normal circumstances, who alone is authorized to exercise the presiding or leadership role in the worship of the Episcopal Church? _____

_____ What exception is made to this rule (see B.C.P., p. 13)? _____

_____

_____

9. The Christian Year is divided into seven basic seasons of observance. What is the proper order of these seasons (see B.C.P., pp. 31-32)?

    a. _____      e. _____

    b. _____      f. _____

    c. _____      g. _____

    d. _____

10. In addition to the aforementioned seasons, what other two special units of yearly division are provided as essential parts of the Christian Year (see B.C.P., pp. 32-33)?

    a. _____      b. _____

11. For all occasions and days within the Christian Year, there is appointed a "Proper." Of what three parts does a Proper consist (see B.C.P., p. 158)?

a. _____

b. _____

c. _____

12. Propers are also appointed for the Common of Saints and for other Various Occasions (not mentioned above) that may arise, subject, however, to the rules of the Calendar of the Church Year. Name any three of each (see B.C.P., pp. 195-210 and 246-61).

a. Common of Saints: _____; _____;

_____

b. Various Occasions: _____; _____;

_____

13. The "Collect" part of the Proper, which sets forth the prayer theme for the day or occasion being celebrated, is provided in both traditional and contemporary language. Where is each to be found?

a. Traditional: _____

b. Contemporary: _____

14. The "Proper Preface" part of the Proper, which further expands on the theme of the Eucharist being celebrated, is also provided in both traditional and contemporary language. Where is each to be found?

a. Traditional: _____

b. Contemporary: _____

15. The "Psalms and Lessons" part of the Proper, which express the biblical theme of the day or occasion being observed, and which may be read in a number of authorized translations (See Title II., Canon 2), are set forth in a "three-year cycle"

for use at the _____ and in a "two-year cycle" for use with

the _____. Where is each to be found?

a. Eucharist: _____

b. Daily Office: _____

_____

16. "Proper Liturgies," or special services, are provided for six important days of great religious significance within the Christian Year. For what special days are these Proper Liturgies provided?

a. _____    d. _____

b. _____    e. _____

c. _____    f. _____

17. The Pastoral Offices represent those services that identify the ministry of the church with some of the more important occasions and events that may take place in our lives and for which and through which the blessing of the Lord is given. What are the Pastoral Offices?

a. _____

b. _____

c. _____

d. _____

e. _____

f. _____

_____

g. _____

h. _____

i. _____

j. _____

k. _____

l. _____

18. The Episcopal Services, with two exceptions wherein the bishop may delegate the presiding role (see B.C.P., pp. 548 and 558), are those services of the church over which only a bishop can preside. What are the Episcopal Services?

a. _____

b. _____

c. _____

d. _____

e. _____

f. _____

What Pastoral Office is also, technically, an Episcopal Service, in that only a

bishop is empowered to preside? _____.

19. What most essential and helpful form is provided in the Book of Common Prayer
wherein you will find a comprehensive summary of the teachings, belief, and

practice of the Episcopal Church (see B.C.P., p. 845)? _____

_____

What additional section of the Book of Common Prayer adds further background

to the teachings of our church (see B.C.P., p. 864)? _____

_____

20. The Book of Common Prayer, in specifying the music of the church to be used
in conjunction with its services (see B.C.P., p. 14), refers in great measure to what
other major book authorized for use by the General Convention of the Episcopal

Church? _____. In looking through your Hymnal you will
note a wide variety of dates, from ancient to modern, and material from a diversity

of _____, which represents an effort to reflect the pluralistic
nature of the Church. Further, it should be noted that the use of musical instru-

ments, in addition to the organ, is _____.

21. What are three specific ways in which our Hymnal correlates with the structure
and usage of the Book of Common Prayer?

a. _____

_____

b. _____

_____

c. _____

_____

22. With respect to how music is used in the church, Title II., Canon 6., Sec. 1
states: "It shall be the duty of every Minister to see that music is used as an

_____ for the glory of God and as a help to the people in
their worship in accordance with the Book of Common Prayer and as authorized

by the General Convention of this Church. To this end the _____

shall have _____ authority in the administration of matters pertaining to music. In fulfilling this responsibility the Minister shall seek

assistance from _____. Together they shall see

that music is appropriate to the _____ in which it is used.''

23. Just as the Episcopal Church has a Standing Liturgical Commission that, among other things, "collects and collates material bearing upon future revisions of the Book of Common Prayer," so too our church has a group that "collects and collates material bearing upon future revisions of the Hymnal." What is the

name of this group? _____.
You may write to either of these groups at the Episcopal Church Center, 815 Second Avenue, New York, NY 10017.

*Supplementary Information on Church Music*
*of Benefit to Parishioners, Clergy, and Musicians*

**Of Special Note**

The following special publications, as well as other helpful books, are available from the Church Hymnal Corporation, 800 Second Avenue, New York, NY 10017-4754:

*The Hymnal (1982) Companion.* Contains essays on important facets of hymnody, as well as individual entries on all hymn texts and tunes. Additionally, biographies of all authors, translators, composers, and arrangers are included. This book is a must!

*Hymnal Studies Seven.* An exhaustive index of organ music based on tunes found in the Hymnal 1982. Each alphabetical tune entry is followed by a comprehensive list of related organ works, organized by composer and graded according to difficulty. Great assistance to organists in selecting repertoire related to hymnody used in the liturgy.

*Hymnal Studies Eight.* All hymn texts based on Scripture are listed in biblical order. Also, there is a table showing the part of the Lectionary cycle in which that particular scripture passage is used. An invaluable addition to the library of all musicians and clergy.

## Service Music and Principles of Chanting

Because many parts of our services are designed to be sung by the minister and people, instead of always being said (see B.C.P., p. 14), you will find choral arrangements for these parts of our services numbered as S 1 through S 288 in the Hymnal 1982.

## Indices

On pages 932-60 of the Hymnal 1982, you will find the following helpful information: (a) Copyright Acknowlegments for Service Music, 931; (b) Copyright Acknowledgments for Hymns, 932; (c) Authors, Translators, and Sources, 936; (d) Composers, Arrangers, and Sources for Service Music, 941; (e) Composers, Arrangers, and Sources for Hymns, 943; (f) Index of Tune Names, 949; and (g) Index of First Lines, 954.

# THE TITLES OF THE SEASONS
## Sundays and Major Holy Days observed in this Church throughout the Year

**Advent Season**

The First Through the Fourth Sundays in Advent

**Christmas Season**

The Nativity of Our Lord Jesus Christ, or Christmas Day — December 25

The First Sunday after Christmas Day

The Holy Name of Our Lord Jesus Christ — January 1

The Second Sunday after Christmas Day

**Epiphany Season**

The Epiphany, or the Manifestation of Christ to the Gentiles — January 6

The First Sunday after The Epiphany, The Baptism of Our Lord Jesus Christ

The Second through the Eighth Sundays after The Epiphany

The Last Sunday after the Epiphany

**Lenten Season**

The First Day of Lent, commonly called Ash Wednesday

The First through the Fifth Sundays in Lent

**Holy Week**

The Sunday of the Passion: Palm Sunday

Monday, Tuesday, and Wednesday in Holy Week

Maundy Thursday

Good Friday

Holy Saturday

**Easter Season**

Easter Eve

The Sunday of the Resurrection, or Easter Day

Monday, Tuesday, Wednesday, Thursday, Friday, and Saturday in Easter Week

The Second through the Sixth Sundays of Easter

Ascension Day

The Seventh Sunday of Easter

The Day of Pentecost, or Whitsunday

**The Season of Pentecost**

The First Sunday after Pentecost: Trinity Sunday

The Second through the Twenty-Seventh Sundays after Pentecost

The Last Sunday after Pentecost, or the Sunday before Advent

**HOLY DAYS**

St. Andrew the Apostle — November 30

St. Thomas the Apostle — December 21

The Nativity of Our Lord Jesus Christ — December 25

St. Stephen, Deacon and Martyr — December 26

St. John, Apostle and Evangelist — December 27

The Holy Innocents — December 28

The Holy Name of Our Lord Jesus Christ — January 1

The Epiphany of Our Lord Jesus Christ — January 6

The Confession of St. Peter the Apostle — January 18

The Conversion of St. Paul the Apostle — January 25

The Presentation of Our Lord Jesus Christ in the Temple — February 2

St. Matthias the Apostle — February 24

St. Joseph — March 19

The Annunciation of Our Lord Jesus Christ to the Blessed Virgin Mary — March 25

St. Mark the Evangelist — April 25

St. Philip and St. James, Apostles — May 1

The Visitation of the Blessed Virgin Mary — May 31

St. Barnabas the Apostle — June 11

The Nativity of St. John the Baptist — June 24

St. Peter and St. Paul, Apostles — June 29

Independence Day — July 4

St. Mary Magdalene — July 22

St. James the Apostle — July 25

The Transfiguration of Our Lord Jesus Christ — August 6

St. Mary the Virgin, Mother of Our Lord Jesus Christ — August 15

St. Bartholomew the Apostle — August 24

Holy Cross Day — September 14

St. Matthew, Apostle and Evangelist — September 21

St. Michael and All Angels — September 29

St. Luke the Evangelist — October 18

St. James of Jerusalem, Brother of Our Lord Jesus Christ, and Martyr — October 23

St. Simon and St. Jude, Apostles — October 28

All Saints — November 1

# NOTES

# NOTES

# 6. The Creeds: Historic Statements of Belief

1. The Episcopal Church gives primary allegiance to two great historic confessions or statements of belief that date back to the early centuries of the Christian Church. What are the names of these two creeds?

   a. _____     b. _____

2. The English word *creed*, derived from the Latin word *credo,* means _____. In the sense and manner in which it is used by the Church, what is a creed?

   _____

   _____

   _____

3. What is the origin of the Apostles' Creed? _____

   _____

   _____

   _____

   _____

4. What is the origin of the Nicene Creed? _____

   _____

   _____

   _____

   _____

5. In terms of liturgical usage, while the Nicene Creed is said on Sundays and other

   major feasts at the _____ as a collective affirmation ("We"; the use of "I" is permitted in the Holy Eucharist, Rite One) of belief of the

   _____ Church, the Apostles' Creed is said in our daily worship

   and represents the _____ statement and affirmation of our belief, in that it continually calls to mind the commitment made at our

   _____. On what three occasions, other than in Daily Office, does the 1979 Book of Common Prayer give us an opportunity to renew this Baptismal Convenant?

   a. _____

   b. _____

c. _____

_____

6. The following is a breakdown of your Baptismal Covenant (the Apostles' Creed) into its significant or major phrases (the traditional rendering is still permissible in Rite One of Daily Morning Prayer and Daily Evening Prayer). In your own words attempt to define what each of these phrases means.

a. I believe in: _____

_____

_____

b. God, the Father: _____

_____

_____

c. Almighty: _____

_____

d. Creator of heaven and earth: _____

_____

_____

e. I believe in Jesus Christ: _____

_____

_____

f. His only Son: _____

_____

_____

g. Our Lord: _____

_____

_____

h. He was conceived by the power of the Holy Spirit and born of the Virgin Mary:

_____

_____

i. He suffered under Pontius Pilate: _____

_____

_____

j. Was crucified, died, and was buried: _____

_____

_____

k. He descended to the dead: _____

_____

_____

l. On the third day he rose again: _____

_____

_____

m. He ascended into heaven: _____

_____

_____

n. And is seated at the right hand of the Father: _____

_____

_____

o. He will come again to judge the living and the dead: _____

_____

_____

_____

p. I believe in the Holy Spirit: _____

_____

_____

q. The holy catholic Church: _____

_____

_____

_____

_____

r. The communion of saints: _____

_____

_____

_____

s. The forgiveness of sins: _____

_____

_____

_____

t. The resurrection of the body, and the life everlasting: _____

_____

_____

_____

7. Western Christendom, most notably the Roman Catholic church and the Anglican communion, have accepted and made use, from time to time, of a third major creed (see B.C.P., p. 864) that dates from the late fourth century. What is the name

of this creed? _____

_____

This creed is an exposition of the doctrines of the _____ and

the _____. What pronouncement is made in this creed that

is not made in either the Apostles' or Nicene creeds? _____

_____

_____

8. What is the name of the church council held in A.D. 451 that defined the divine and human natures in the Person of Christ (see B.C.P., p. 864)? _____ _____. This council said that Jesus is truly _____ and truly _____, i.e., he is _____ person recognized in _____ natures. What are four significant words that define the uniting of these two natures in the one Person of Christ?

a. _____    c. _____

b. _____    d. _____

9. What are the "Articles of Religion" (see B.C.P., p. 867)? _____

_____

_____

10. The Chicago-Lambeth Quadrilateral (see B.C.P., p. 876), being a consensus of the Episcopal Church's General Convention of 1886 and the Lambeth Conference of 1888, sets forth the Anglican position on the principal elements that are necessary for Christian unity. What are these four essential requirements?

a. _____

_____

b. _____

_____

c. _____

_____

d. _____

_____

# NOTES

# NOTES

# NOTES

# 7. Moral and Ethical Living

1. St. Augustine, the great theologian of the early Christian Church, once summarized how a Christian ought to approach life's moral and ethical decisions by saying, _____ In giving this advice St. Augustine was making the profound observation that if one's heart and _____ are truly in accord with God's will, then one's _____ will be compassionate, just, and in accordance with the moral imperatives set forth in the _____.

2. The Ten Commandments, found in the Bible in Exod. 20:2-17 and in Deut. 5:6-21, were originally received from God by _____ on Mount Sinai. What is the basic purpose of the Ten Commandments? _____

_____

_____

_____

_____

3. In their proper order and sequence, write out the Ten Commandments (use contemporary translation on B.C.P., p. 350). And then, immediately following each commandment, spell out the ethical implications that God is making in each commandment about your relationship with him and your fellow human beings. You may wish to use the Book of Common Prayer, pages 847-48, as a guide. Make a special effort to be specific in your answers.

    I. _____

    _____

    _____

    Means: _____

    _____

    II. _____

    _____

    Means: _____

III. _____

_____

Means: _____

_____

_____

IV. _____

_____

Means: _____

_____

_____

V. _____

Means: _____

_____

_____

VI. _____

Means: _____

_____

_____

_____

VII. _____

Means: _____

_____

VIII. _____

Means: _____

_____

IX. _____

Means: _____

_____

_____

X. _____

_____

Means: _____

_____

_____

4. In terms of liturgical format, how does the Book of Common Prayer suggest that the Ten Commandments be used?

a. _____

_____

_____

b. _____

_____

_____

_____

5. When Jesus was asked by the lawyer, in Matt. 22:35-40, which was the "great commandment" in the Law, he summarized the ethical teaching of the Ten Commandments by saying (see B.C.P., p. 851):

a. _____

_____

_____

b. _____

_____

6. Our Lord's Summary of the Law characterizes further the makeup of the Ten Commandments, in that commandments one through four deal with our duty

toward _____ and commandments five through ten spell out

our duty toward our _____.

7. As we live out our lives with the Ten Commandments and Jesus' Summary of the Law as a guide to our ethical behavior, we are encouraged by St. Paul, in Gal. 5:22-23, to base our interpersonal conduct upon the following nine virtues, which are often referred to as the "fruits of the Spirit":

a. _____      f. _____

b. _____      g. _____

c. _____      h. _____

d. _____      i. _____

e. _____

Which of these virtues is the most difficult for you to carry out in your own life, and what does this tell you about yourself?

_____

_____

_____

_____

8. In Matt. 5:17 Jesus says, "Think not that I have come to abolish the law and the prophets; I have come not to abolish them but to _____ them." This new way of applying ethical and moral standards to the human situation enables us to move from an unforgiving and rigid _____ to a compassionate and forgiving _____. This is what St. Paul means when he says in Rom. 6:14 that we are ". . . not under law, but under grace" and again in 2 Cor. 3:6 when he comments that ". . . the written code _____, but the Spirit gives _____."

9. The practical application of the New Testament ethic of living "under grace" and "in the Spirit" means, not only that forgiveness is freely given when we _____, but also that there must always be room for an "understanding flexibility of love" in those difficult and complex ethical dilemmas where _____ and _____ meet face to face. Name three such ethical dilemmas:

a. _____

_____

_____

_____

b. _____

_____

_____

_____

c. _____

_____

_____

_____

_____

# NOTES

# NOTES

# NOTES

# 8. The Personal Devotional Life

1. In John 10:10, Jesus says that he came into this world that we might ". . . have life, and have it abundantly." Accordingly, the person who wishes to achieve and maintain a wholesome balance, maturity, and resilient flexibility in their life, i.e., come to know and experience the "abundant life," must make a concerted effort

   to _____ regularly in five essential ways. These ways are:

   a. _____          d. _____

   b. _____          e. _____

   c. _____

2. When we "work out spiritually" to enhance our relationship with God and one another, we engage in the practice of prayer. Indeed, the Book of Common Prayer (see B.C.P., p. 856) defines prayer, in its broadest sense, as the response (an action or movement) that one makes to God, expressed with or without words, and

   manifested by the person's _____ and _____.
   What are the seven basic ways through which one may express thoughts and deeds in prayer (see B.C.P., pp. 856-57)?

   a. _____          e. _____

   b. _____          f. _____

   c. _____          g. _____

   d. _____

3. What essential phrase (or intention or verbalization) in the offering of a prayer makes that prayer a truly Christian prayer?

   _____

   _____

4. When the disciples said to Jesus, "Lord, teach us to pray," our Lord taught them

   what is known as the _____. The Book of Common Prayer, following the pattern set forth in the Bible in Matt. 6:4-13 and

   Luke 11:2-4, presents _____ versions of the Lord's Prayer (compare B.C.P., pp. 132 and 153 with p. 311; the reference here is not to traditional or contemporary language). What is the essential difference between these two versions?

   _____

_____

_____

5. In the following breakdown of the Lord's Prayer into its major phrases, attempt in your own words to define the meaning of each phrase.

a. Our Father: _____

_____

_____

b. Who art in heaven [Our Father in heaven]: _____

_____

_____

_____

c. Hallowed be thy [your] name: _____

_____

_____

d. Thy [your] kingdom come: _____

_____

e. Thy [your] will be done, on earth as it is in heaven [on earth as in heaven]:

_____

_____

_____

f. Give us this day [today] our daily bread: _____

_____

_____

g. And forgive us our trespasses [forgive us our sins], as we forgive those who

trespass [sin] against us: _____

_____

_____

h. And lead us not into temptation [save us from the time of trial], but [and] deliver

us from evil: _____

i. For thine is the kingdom, and the power, and the glory, for ever and ever [for the kingdom, the power, and the glory are yours, now and forever]. Amen:

_____

_____

_____

6. In the course of his ministry Jesus talked many other times about the subject and nature of prayer. List six of these instances (chapter and verse).

   a. _____        d. _____

   b. _____        e. _____

   c. _____        f. _____

7. In accordance with our Lord's teaching that we offer prayer, engage in acts of charity, and exercise godly discipline each day of our life, the Episcopal Church observes "Days of Special Devotion" (see B.C.P., p. 17) upon which we are encouraged to practice acts of discipline and self-denial. Basically stated, what are these days?

   a. _____

   _____

   b. _____

   _____

(**NOTE:** See special exceptions to this, B.C.P., p. 17.)

8. As an act of special devotion many persons find it helpful, from time to time, to make a private confession of their sins to a priest. This sacramental rite,

traditionally called _____, is found in the Pastoral Office

entitled, _____. The rationale of this

sacramental rite, under which _____ is morally absolute for the confessor (see B.C.P., p. 446), is best explained in the Exhortation, which reads (see B.C.P., p. 317): "And if, in your preparation, you need help and counsel, then go and open your grief to a discreet and understanding priest, and confess your sins, that you may receive the benefit of absolution, and spiritual counsel and advice; to the removal of scruple and doubt, the assurance of pardon, and the strengthening of your faith."

9. As another means of furthering your personal devotional life, The Book of Common Prayer provides a special section in which you will find various prayers, in Collect form, that relate to many of the circumstances that will arise in your

   life. What and where is this found? _____

   _____

   (**NOTE:** A complete subject index to all the prayers in the Book of Common Prayer is found at the back of this book.)

10. The Hymnal of the church also provides a wealth of devotional material, much like the Psalter, in that the words of many of the hymns can be used profitably

    alone, without a musical setting, as _____.
    Good examples of this are the following:
    a. Hymn 503 as a prayer for inspiration and divine aid.
    b. Hymn 337 as a prayer before receiving Holy Communion.
    c. Hymn 312 as a prayer after receiving Holy Communion.
    d. Hymn 707 as a prayer of dedication at any time.
    e. Hymn 694 as a prayer for God's presence in your life.
    f. Hymn 416 as a general thanksgiving.
    g. Hymn 671 as a meditation on the meaning of God's forgiveness.
    h. Hymn 44 as a prayer before going to bed.

    (**NOTE:** Look through the Hymnal and find some prayer-hymns that you like and find to be helpful in your own private devotions.)

*How to Compose a Collect*

What follows are the five basic steps in composing a traditionally structured prayer or Collect, whether the language used is traditional (thee-thine) or contemporary (you-your). After studying these five steps, use your own creative imagination, feelings, and thoughts and write a number of prayers in your own words in the space provided. (**NOTE:** for free-verse prayer composition, follow the pattern of the prayer-hymns that you have found to be helpful).

**Opening Ascription**

This should be addressed to God in one fashion or another. Some of the more characteristic opening ascriptions are as follows: Almighty God; O Lord; O Almighty and everlasting Father; Lord God Almighty; Gracious God; Everliving God; Lord God of power and might; Blessed Lord.

**Descriptive Clause**

This clause should tell something about the God whom you have addressed in your opening, i.e., it may describe one of his characteristics, tell where he is, relate how he deals with us, etc. Examples of such clauses are as follows: who has taught us that all our doings without charity are worth nothing; Look with pity upon the sorrows of thy [your] servant [name] for whom our prayers are offered; By thy [your] Spirit lift us, we pray thee [you] to thy [your] presence, where we may be still and know that thou art [you are] God; We commend this nation to thy [your] merciful care, that, being guided by thy [your] Providence, we may dwell secure in thy [your] peace; etc.

## Basic Statement

This is the central part of the prayer and may express adoration, praise, thanksgiving, penitence, oblation, intercession, or petition. Examples of these statements are as follows: Let thy [your] Spirit go forth, that it may renew the face of the earth; Look with pity upon the sorrows of thy [your] servant [name] for whom our prayers are offered; By thy [your] Spirit lift us, we pray thee [you], to thy [your] presence, where we may be still and know that thou art [you are] God; We commend this nation to thy [your] merciful care, that, being guided by thy [your] Providence, we may dwell secure in thy [your] peace; etc.

## Intercessory Close

Because Jesus Christ has come to us that we might have access to God the Father, the closing of the prayer beseeches or asks Jesus Christ to bring our prayer to God the Father on our behalf. Some characteristic closing statements are as follows: through Jesus Christ our Lord; through our Mediator and Advocate, Jesus Christ; through Jesus Christ our Lord, who liveth [lives] and reigneth [reigns] with thee [you] and the Holy Ghost [Holy Spirit], one God, world without end; etc.

## Punctuation—Ending

A comma follows the Opening Ascription. A semicolon follows the Descriptive Clause. The Basic Statement begins with a capital letter and ends with a semicolon. The Intercessory Close begins uncapitalized and ends with a period. Then comes the word *Amen,* which means "so be it" or "I agree."

*Space Below for Traditional Prayer Composition*

*Space Below for Contemporary Prayer Composition*

# NOTES

# NOTES

# 9. The Daily Office

1. The Christian community, from earliest of times in the second century, gathered for a time of prayer and praise in both the morning and evening. Our prayer book term *Daily Office* refers specifically to two services of prayer and praise that are set forth to be read by the Christian community every day of the year. What are these two services?

   a. _____

   b. _____

2. The services of Daily Morning and Evening Prayer are alike in that they each provide for an optional beginning that includes three basic elements of worship. These are:

   a. _____

   b. _____    c. _____
   What additional optional beginning is provided for the service of Daily Evening

   Prayer (see B.C.P., pp. 61 and 115?) _____

   _____

   _____

   _____

3. The services of Daily Morning and Evening Prayer are alike also in that they each require a liturgical format that includes three basic parts or service divisions. These are:

   a. _____

   b. _____    c. _____

4. In addition to the Gloria Patri, what elements comprise the Invitatory and Psalter in Daily Morning Prayer (see B.C.P., pp. 42-46 and 80-84)?

   a. _____

   b. _____

   c. _____
   What takes the place of the Venite or Jubilate during Easter Week and may further

   be used until the Day of Pentecost (see B.C.P., pp. 45-46 and 83)? _____

   _____

5. In addition to the Gloria Patri, what elements comprise the Invitatory and Psalter in Daily Evening Prayer (see B.C.P., pp. 63-64 and 117-18)?

   a. _____

   _____

   b. _____

6. The Lessons that are read in Daily Morning and Evening Prayer (see B.C.P., pp. 934-1001), when two are included, follow the pattern of the First Lesson being

   taken from the _____ and the Second Lesson

   from the _____. When, however, three Lessons are

   read, or the Holy Eucharist is to follow, a reading from the _____
   must always be included. Immediately following the reading of each Lesson, what may be done to provide the congregation with an opportunity to meditate on what

   they have heard? _____

7. After each Lesson is read in both Daily Morning and Evening Prayer, what is

   designated to be said or sung (see B.C.P., pp. 84 and 119)? _____.
   Of all of these Canticles, based directly or indirectly in the Scriptures, which three are "Gospel" Canticles?

   a. _____        c. _____

   b. _____

8. Each Canticle has a Latin name that, when translated into English, always comes

   out to be _____.
   Under special circumstances, however, what may be substituted for any Canticle

   (see B.C.P., p. 142)? _____

9. The Prayers at Daily Morning and Evening Prayer, as a normal rule, consist of four essential things. They are:

   a. _____

   b. _____

   c. _____

   d. _____

   _____

10. What are the three primary sources from which these authorized intercessions and/or thanksgiving are usually drawn?

   a. _____

   b. _____

   c. _____

11. During the above mentioned intercessions and/or thanksgivings, special opportunity may be given for two additional facets of devotional expression on the part of the congregation. These are (see B.C.P., p. 142):

   a. _____

   _____

   b. _____

12. A sermon or meditation at services of Daily Morning and Evening Prayer is optional at the discretion of the minister. On occasion, what special form may the meditation take (see B.C.P., p. 142)? _____

   _____ What else is optional and at the

   discretion of the minister (see B.C.P., p. 142)? _____

13. The services of Daily Morning and Evening Prayer may be used also in the context of the Holy Eucharist as the principal service of worship on Sundays or other major feasts. When this is done, the Daily Office is used as what (see B.C.P., p. 142)? _____. Under these circumstances, the Nicene Creed takes the place of the Apostles' Creed and three additional things must be included. They are (see B.C.P., p. 142):

   a. _____

   _____

   b. _____

   c. _____

   _____

14. In addition to Daily Morning and Evening Prayer, that section of the Book of Common Prayer entitled "The Daily Office" also contains four other services of daily devotion. What are they?

a. _____

b. _____

c. _____

d. _____

_____

15. The service "An Order of Worship for the Evening" provides for corporate or home worship that may be used in three basic ways. These are (see B.C.P., p. 108):

a. _____

_____

b. _____

_____

c. _____

_____

16. The service "An Order for Compline" (see B.C.P., pp. 127-35) may be used in both corporate or home worship and was originally the last form of prayer that was offered in the daily monastic office. When is this service most appropriately used?

_____

_____

17. The form "Daily Devotions for Individuals and Families" provides a shortened form for personal and corporate prayer used most appropriately in the home at four specific times. They are (see B.C.P., pp. 136-40):

a. _____    c. _____

b. _____    d. _____

18. "The Great Litany," which is especially appropriate for use during Lent and on Rogation Days, as well as during Advent, is one of the great responsorial prayers of the Church. Traditionally, it is often said or sung in procession. In terms of liturgical format, where may the Great Litany be used (see B.C.P., p. 148)?

a. _____

b. _____

c. _____

19. The Great Litany consists of four basic parts that emphasize different aspects of our responsive prayer. These are:

a. _____

_____

b. _____

c. _____

_____

d. _____

20. The Book of Common Prayer contains four other litanies, which, although they are used primarily for special and specific occasions, may be used at other times and provide great devotional benefit. What is the name of each of these litanies and where may each be found?

a. _____

b. _____

c. _____

_____

d. _____

# NOTES

# NOTES

# NOTES

# 10. Church Customs and Symbolism

1. The Preface to the Book of Common Prayer of 1789, in speaking of the benefits to be gained from the openness and comprehensive nature of the Anglican tradition, states (see B.C.P., p. 9):

    It is a most invaluable part of that blessed "liberty wherewith Christ has made us free," that in his worship

    _____ forms and usages

    may without offence be _____,
    provided the substance of the Faith be

    kept _____.

2. Accordingly, while the Episcopal Church adheres to the standardized format of liturgical services found in the Book of Common Prayer, the _____ manner in which these services are conducted will vary according to the

    _____ of the respective parish, as will the _____ practices of the worshipers in these services.

3. The right and privilege of "personal preference" in devotional practices is a

    highly valued _____ of our Anglican heritage and reflects

    God's creation of each of us as equal but _____ in his sight. Therefore, differences in devotional practices should never be construed as either a lack of reverence, on the one hand, or a higher degree of spirituality, on the other. As Episcopalians, we are encouraged to practice those devotional customs

    that are expressive of and _____ to our own spirituality and to respect that same right in others.

4. The following devotional practices and/or customs are often observed in the Episcopal Church. What is the practice and/or custom that is being described?

    a. _____: Action done in the blessing of things such as wedding rings, palms, houses, etc. Symbolizes purity, new life, and new beginnings. When this action includes the whole congregation, it symbolizes a forging of the relationship between our baptism and what we are doing in the Eucharist.

    b. _____: A personal reaffirmation of our baptism in which we offer our prayers, praises, and labors (or whatever else we are about to undertake) in the Name of the Father, and of the Son, and of the Holy Spirit. Some worshipers upon entering church cross themselves with Holy Water that is provided in a receptacle called a "stoup" located in the narthex of some churches.

**NOTE:** At the reading of the Gospel some people will make the Sign of the Cross on their forehead, then on their lips, and then over their heart. The symbolism is that we ask God to indwell our minds, speak through our lips, and enkindle our hearts so that we may become better and more effective

_____ and witnesses to Christ's love in the world.

    c. _____: Kneeling on the right knee momentarily to show special devotion and recognition of our Lord's presence in the Blessed Sacrament, as well as acknowledging the mystery of the Incarnation when this expression is made in the Nicene Creed.

    d. _____: An act of personal reverence to the cross and/or the altar, as well as another way of expressing devotional recognition of our Lord's presence in the Blessed Sacrament.

    e. _____: An ancient ritual practice used to symbolize the offering up of our prayers and praises most generally at festival Eucharists, as well as to signify the blessings and setting apart of things, much as Holy Water is often used. Reference to this is made in Ps. 141:2.

5. In many Episcopal churches, our Lord's presence in the Blessed Sacrament, which has been "reserved" in the "aumbry," is made known symbolically to the congregation by means of a large and prominently displayed candle that burns continuously. This candle, which is housed in either a red or clear globe, is known

as a _____.

6. The altar hangings and the vestments of the clergy, while varying from the plain to the highly ornamented, generally follow a traditional pattern in terms of liturgical colors, depending upon the season or occasion. These colors are as follows:

    a. _____ at Christmas, Easter, Ascensiontide, Transfiguration, weddings, and baptisms. The colors symbolize joy. Often used now at burials to symbolize the joy of the resurrection.

    b. _____ at Pentecost and on saints' days (martyrs only). Red is used also for confirmations and ordinations. It symbolizes the tongues of fire of the Holy Spirit, as well as blood.

    c. _____ during Advent and Lent, as well as on Ember and Rogation days. It is a penitential color. Purple is sometimes used for burials.

d. _____ during the seasons of Pentecost and Epiphany. It is the universal color and symbolizes creation, nature, and hope.

e. _____ on Good Friday. It denotes grief.

7. What do the following designations denote?

    a. The Most Reverend _____

    b. The Right Reverend _____

    c. The Very Reverend _____

    _____

    d. The Venerable _____

    e. The Reverend Canon _____

    f. The Reverend _____

8. What do the following degree designations denote?

    a. M.Div. _____

    b. S.T.M. _____

    c. S.T.D. _____

    d. Th.D. _____

    e. D.D. _____

    f. D.Min. _____

9. The most important of all Christian symbols is the cross. It is a constant reminder to us of Christ's _____ and _____ and _____. Therefore, in addition to the "plain or unadorned cross" that you will see in many churches, some churches choose, because of the intensified symbolism, to employ two other distinctive cross designs. What is each of these designs called?

    a. _____: Jesus hanging on the cross with only a cloth about his loins, representing and reminding us of his suffering and death on our behalf.

    b. _____: Our Lord, Christ the King, upright on the cross, with arms outstretched, in royal garments, representing and symbolizing his Resurrection and promise to us of eternal life.

10. What is the meaning of the following symbols that are commonly used in the Christian Church?

a.

_____

_____

_____

_____

b.

_____

_____

_____

_____

_____

c.

_____

_____

_____

_____

_____

d.

_____

_____

_____

_____

e.

_____

_____

_____

_____

_____

f.

_____

_____

_____

_____

g.

IXΘYC

_____

_____

_____

_____

_____

_____

_____

_____

(**NOTE:** The symbols used are taken from W.E. Post, *Saints, Signs, and Symbols* [Harrisburg, PA: Morehouse Publishing, rev. ed. 1974]. Used by permission.)

# Some
# Sacramental
# Rites

# NOTES

# NOTES

## 11. Sacraments and Ministry

1. Sacraments constitute concrete means through which God's grace or favor is shown to us. As such, sacraments form the basis of the faith, life, worship, and ministry of the Episcopal Church. How may the sacraments be defined (see B.C.P., p. 857)?

Sacraments are the outward and visible _____

of an inward and spiritual _____, given

by _____ as sure and certain means by

which we _____ that grace.

2. What are the two "sacraments of the Gospel" that Christ has given to his Church (see B.C.P., p. 858)?

a. _____          b. _____

3. The outward and visible sign in the sacrament of Holy Baptism is the _____.
What, then, is the inward and spiritual grace or favor received (see B.C.P., p. 858)?

a. _____

_____

b. _____

c. _____

d. _____

4. The outward and visible sign in the sacrament of the Holy Eucharist is the

_____ and _____. What, then, is the inward

and spiritual grace or favor received (see B.C.P., p. 859)? _____

_____

_____

5. In our reception of Christ's lifegiving presence in the sacrament of the Holy Eucharist we receive certain specific benefits. They are (see B.C.P., pp. 859-60) as follows:

a. _____

b. _____

_____

c. _____

_____

6. The Episcopal Church, like her sister churches in the Catholic tradition, has, under the guidance of the Holy Spirit, continued to administer five "sacramental rites" through which God's grace and favor is conferred in sacramental action. These are defined as follows in the Catechism (see B.C.P., pp. 860-61):

a. _____ This is the rite in which we express a mature commitment to Christ and receive strength from the Holy Spirit through prayer and the laying on of hands by a bishop.

b. _____ This is the rite of Christian marriage in which a woman and man enter into a life-long union, make vows before God and the Church, and receive the grace and blessing of God to help them fulfill their vows. What three requirements does the Episcopal Church make of those desiring this sacramental rite (see B.C.P., p. 422)?

(1) _____

(2) _____

(3) _____

_____

c. _____ This is the rite in which God gives authority and the grace of the Holy Spirit to those being made bishops, priests, and deacons, through prayer and the laying on of hands by bishops.

d. _____ This is the rite in which those who repent of their sins may confess them to God in the presence of a priest and receive the assurance of pardon and the grace of absolution.

e. _____ This is the rite of anointing the sick with oil, or the laying on of hands, by which God's grace is given for the healing of spirit, mind, and body. In which of the Pastoral Offices is the sacramental

rite to be found? _____

7. While they are not, however, rites of a sacramental nature, "Ministration at the Time of Death" and "The Burial of the Dead" are rites of great pastoral significance in that they convey, in the midst of human sorrow and grief, the joy of the

Easter promise that finds its meaning in the _____ of Christ. What special features do these two Pastoral Offices provide (see B.C.P., pp. 462, 465, 466, 470, 487, 494, and 503)?

a. _____

_____

b. _____

_____

c. _____

d. _____

e. _____

8. The rubrics and directives in "An Order for Marriage" and "An Order for Burial," in addition to allowing for creative liturgical design, also provide, if so desired—

and this is implied—for the continued usage of what? _____

_____

_____

9. The Pastoral Office of "A Thanksgiving for the Birth or Adoption of a Child" suggests that parents and other family members, as soon as is convenient after the birth or adoption of a child, should come to the church for two purposes. These are (see B.C.P., p. 439):

a. _____

b. _____

(**NOTE:** If desired, however, a briefer form of this service may be used in the hospital or at home.)

10. The Episcopal Church, in accordance with the apostolic tradition and the Catholic faith, has three distinct orders of ordained ministers called by God to special responsibilities in the church. In order of rank or ecclesiastical function (lowest to highest) they are:

a. _____    c. _____

b. _____
Where is the rationale for this threefold order of ministry explained in the 1979

*Book of Common Prayer*? _____

_____

11. What is the specific work, function, and ministry of a bishop (see B.C.P., p. 855)?

a. _____

_____

_____

b. _____

_____

c. _____

d. _____

_____

_____

e. _____

f. (Implied, as no other order of minister is empowered to do this) _____

12. What is the specific work, function, and ministry of a priest (see B.C.P., p. 856)?

a. _____

_____

b. _____

_____

c. _____

d. _____

e. _____

_____

13. What is the specific work, function, and ministry of a deacon (see B.C.P., p. 856)?

a. _____

_____

_____

b. _____

_____

_____

14. When a person is presented to the bishop for ordination, whether to the order of bishop, priest, or deacon, the candidate makes the following solemn declaration (see B.C.P., pp. 513, 526, and 538):

> I solemnly declare that I do believe the
> Holy Scriptures of the Old and New Testaments
>
> to be the _____, and
> to contain all things necessary to
> salvation; and I do solemnly engage to
>
> _____ to the doctrine,
> discipline, and worship of The Episcopal
> Church.

15. The pastoral ministry of the Church, in its broadest sense, is a ministry that is shared by all Christians, by virtue of the nature and commitment of their baptism. What are the specific responsibilities of the ministry of the laity (see B.C.P., p. 855)?

   a. _____

   b. _____

   _____

   c. _____

   _____

   _____

   d. _____

   _____

16. As a layperson called by God to "ministry," name three specific ways in which you are currently answering this call in your own life situation. I am:

   a. _____

   _____

   b. _____

   _____

   c. _____

   _____

17. Thus, the ministry of Christ, whether lay or ordained, calls every Christian to the duty of following Christ as the Lord of his or her life, the implication being (see B.C.P., p. 856) that we gather together _____ for corporate worship and to _____ and _____ and _____ for the spread of God's kingdom.

# NOTES

# NOTES

## 12. Holy Baptism and Confirmation

1. In both the Old and New Testaments of Scripture, God consistently uses the medium of _____ as a cleansing and transforming change agent to accomplish his purposes and bring renewal. Name three such dramatic instances (see B.C.P., p. 306):

    a. _____

    _____

    b. _____

    _____

    _____

    c. _____

    _____

2. The Greek word *baptizo,* from which our English word *baptize* is derived, means literally "to _____ or _____ or _____." Therefore, in characteristic fashion, when God chooses to call us into a unique transforming and renewing relationship with him, he again uses the medium of water.

3. The transforming action and renewing event that takes place by the power of the Holy Spirit at one's *baptizo* or "immersing and washing" is known as being _____ and transforms the person from non-Christian "to" Christian. For Episcopalians then, the term *born-again Christian* is theologically redundant and akin to saying "Christian-Christian," for if you have been born again at baptism you "are" a Christian and fully _____ by the Holy Spirit.

    **NOTE:** When self-proclaimed born-again Christians challenge our degree of dedication to the Lord and strength of personal faith, what they are really saying to us is this (and we might learn something by listening): "If you really do have the power of the Holy Spirit in your life, then why do you look and act religiously _____ and spiritually _____ so much of the time!"

4. The Sacrament of Holy Baptism, ordained by Christ, establishes an indissoluble bond between a person and God. As such, Holy Baptism signifies full

_____ into Christ's Body the Church, wherein we are

_____ as God's children and made inheritors of the kingdom

of heaven.

5. What are the three specific things that are required of us at baptism (see B.C.P., p. 858)?

a. _____

b. _____

c. _____

_____

6. When, where, and by whom is baptism most appropriately administered (see B.C.P., pp. 298 and 312)?

a. _____

b. _____

_____

_____

_____

_____

_____

c. _____

_____

7. The blessed water of baptism, which imparts the Holy Spirit, may be used in either of two ways (see B.C.P., p. 307):

a. _____

b. _____

8. What further form is used by the bishop or priest to signify that the newly baptized

person is sealed by the Holy Spirit (see B.C.P., p. 308)? _____

_____. In so doing,

the oil of Chrism, which may be consecrated only by a _____,

may be used.

9. The Episcopal Church requires that each candidate for baptism, whether adult or child, be sponsored by whom (see B.C.P., p. 298)? _____ _____. It is appropriate, when a child is baptized, that parents be included among sponsors or godparents for their own children. True or False (see B.C.P., p. 298)? _____

10. In the baptism of infants and younger children, what are the two promises that the sponsors must make "in their own names" (see B.C.P., p. 302)?

   a. _____

   _____

   b. _____

   _____

   _____

11. At baptism there are the six major promises or vows that sponsors make "on the child's behalf" and that adult candidates make "for themselves." These are (see B.C.P., pp. 302-03):

   a. Renunciation of _____ and all spiritual forces of

   _____ that rebel against God.

   b. Renunciation of _____ that corrupt and destroy the

   _____ of God.

   c. Renunciation of all _____ that draw us from the love of God.

   d. Turning to and _____ of Jesus Christ as Savior.

   e. Putting our whole _____ in Christ's grace and love.

   f. Promising to follow and _____ Christ as Lord.

12. Sponsors, adult candidates, and members of the congregation all affirm and renew something that is called the "Baptismal Covenant." What is this (see B.C.P., pp. 304-05)? _____

   _____

   _____

13. If the bishop is present, prior to the celebration of the Holy Eucharist that follows the service of Holy Baptism, opportunity is given for other persons in the congregation to do one or all of three different things. They are (see B.C.P., pp. 309-10):

a. _____    c. _____

b. _____

14. If an ordained minister cannot be in attendance, a layperson is permitted to baptize under two circumstances, after which he or she must report this act to the priest of the appropriate parish. What are these two circumstances (see B.C.P., pp. 313-14)?

a. _____

_____

b. _____

15. In both conditional and emergency baptism, water is poured on the person to be baptized, but differing words are said. What does one say appropriately in each instance (see B.C.P., p. 313)?

a. Conditional baptism: _____

_____

_____

_____

b. Emergency baptism: _____

_____

_____

_____

16. The Sacramental Rite of Confirmation, which may be a separate service followed

by the Holy Eucharist, can be presided over only by a _____.
Confirmation is defined in the Catechism in the following manner (see B.C.P.,

p. 860): "The rite in which we express a mature _____
to Christ, and receive strength from the Holy Spirit through prayer and the

_____ by a bishop."

17. Who is expected to make this mature and public affirmation of their faith and commitment to the responsibilities of their baptism and to receive the laying on

of hands by a bishop (see B.C.P., p. 412)?

a. _____

_____

_____

b. _____

_____

_____

_____

18. What four requirements does the Episcopal Church make of those who desire to be confirmed (see B.C.P., p. 860)?

a. _____

b. _____

_____

c. _____

d. _____

_____

19. Opportunity is given in the service of confirmation (as it is in Holy Baptism) for

other persons personally to _____ their faith; as well as for

others to be _____ into the Episcopal Church.

20. Another separate service of personal commitment to the work and service of Christ, not, however, having the sacramental importance of confirmation, and in which a bishop need not be present, is provided on page 420 of the *Book of*

*Common Prayer*. What is this service called? _____

_____

Give two occasions upon which you think this service might be an appropriate undertaking in a person's life.

a. _____

b. _____

_____

# NOTES

# NOTES

# NOTES

## 13. The Holy Eucharist

1. The word *Eucharist,* as we have previously noted, is Greek in origin and means

_____. Thus, in the Eucharist, we are giving thanks to God

for enabling us to receive the real and _____ presence of
Christ. Other names for this service, which highlight its many aspects, are (see
B.C.P., p. 859):

   a. _____ This emphasizes that we share in the living
   and holy fellowship of God's Table and are fed and sustained by him, as were
   the disciples themselves.

   b. _____ This stresses the relationship or communion
   that we share in this act with him who is holy—Jesus Christ.

   c. _____ This comes from the Latin phrase *ite missa est*
   ("go, depart, it is done") with which all but the faithful, in the days of the early
   Church, were dismissed just prior to this unique act of Christian worship.

   d. _____ Liturgy denotes a form for public worship.
   Here, we speak of it as divine because God himself actually enters into it.

   e. _____ This proclaims the magnitude of Christ's
   offering of himself for us by his death on the cross and that we, in turn, are
   bound to offer our lives back to him through praise, thanksgiving, and self-
   sacrifice for our fellow human beings.

2. In the Episcopal Church, the Sacrament of the Holy Eucharist, which has been

   ordained by _____, is set forth to be celebrated as the

   _____ of worship on every Sunday and all other major feasts
   (see B.C.P., p. 13). The Book of Common Prayer (see B.C.P., p. 859) says of this

   sacrament that it is "_____ by Christ for the continual

   _____ of his life, death, and resurrection, until his

   _____."

3. What is required of us, on the personal level, before we come to the Holy Eucharist
   (see B.C.P., p. 860)?

   a. _____

   b. _____

   c. _____

4. While only a priest or a bishop may be the celebrant at the Holy Eucharist, the prerogative of being the principal celebrant and preacher is always reserved for

   the _____ when present. In any event, at all celebrations of the Holy Eucharist, it is appropriate that the principal celebrant be assisted by whom (see B.C.P., pp. 322 and 354)?

   a. _____     c. _____

   b. _____

5. Further, the *Book of Common Prayer* directs that it is appropriate for all assisting priests to stand with the celebrant at the altar and to join in three specific acts. These are (see B.C.P., pp. 322 and 354):

   a. _____

   b. _____

   c. _____

6. The Book of Common Prayer provides two services of the Holy Eucharist that are appropriate for celebrations in the church on Sundays and other major feasts. Each of these rites follow the same basic liturgical format by dividing the celebration into the following two distinct parts:

   a. _____

   b. _____

   Celebrations conducted in "traditional language" are referred to as _____, while celebrations making use of "contemporary language" are referred to as

   _____.

7. In addition to the Collect, which sets forth the prayer theme for the particular Eucharist being celebrated, where are the other parts of the Proper, that is, the

   Psalms and Lessons for the particular Eucharist, to be found? _____

   _____

8. Following the reading of the Gospel, the sermon is given. What is the purpose

   of the sermon? _____

   _____

   _____

   _____

9. We, then (on weekdays this is optional), summarize the major tenets of our Christian faith by joining in which historic creed? _____

10. As a part of the Eucharist, normally, we confess our sins and receive absolution. This may be done during the course of the service (see B.C.P., pp. 330 and 359) or by using a special form called _____ at the beginning of the service (see B.C.P., pp. 319 and 351). What special devotional aid is suggested just prior to the confession, both here and in the Daily Office, to aid us in making a more constructive confession? _____

_____

_____

11. What are the three consequences and blessings that are ours when we receive priestly absolution (see B.C.P., pp. 332 and 360)?

a. _____

b. _____

c. _____

_____

12. A major part of the Eucharist consists of the intercessions that are offered, called "The Prayers of the People." While those printed in Rite One differ in form from those on pages 383-93, for whom are the prayers always offered (see B.C.P., p. 383)?

a. _____

_____

b. _____

c. _____

d. _____

e. _____

f. _____

_____

(**NOTE:** If the Great Litany is used before the Eucharist, the Prayers of the People may be omitted.)

13. What other services may be used, "omitting the Prayers of the People," in place of "all" that precedes the offertory in either Rite One or Rite Two?

a. _____

b. _____

c. _____

d. _____

e. _____

f. _____

g. _____

h. _____

(**NOTE:** Remember that when Daily Morning or Evening Prayer are used as the "Liturgy of the Word" in either Rite One or Rite Two of the Holy Eucharist, the Prayers of the People must be included, as well as a sermon (implied), a Gospel reading, and the Nicene Creed.)

14. An ancient form of greeting, expressing the love and joy shared and felt in the Christian community, is said or passed between those who are present at the

Eucharist. What is this called? _____

15. At the offertory, representatives of the congregation bring forward three things to be presented and placed upon the altar, each of which will be blessed and put to a new and holy use by God. What are these three things that are offered (see B.C.P., pp 333 and 361)?

a. _____    c. _____

b. _____

16. The whole liturgical action beginning with the Sursum Corda and concluding with

the great Amen just prior to the Lord's Prayer is known as the _____

_____.

(**NOTE:** Rite One provides one alternative Eucharistic Prayer on p. 343; Rite Two provides three alternative Eucharistic Prayers on pp. 369-77.)

17. The Sursum Corda is a Latin expression that means _____

_____.

The significance of this phrase points to the joy, happiness, and lifting of our spirits we experience knowing and anticipating the great miracle that is about to take place in the _____. This joy is further expanded in the Sanctus, for here we realize that in what we are now doing on earth, we are also being joined by whom? _____

18. The climax of the Eucharist takes place in that part of the Eucharistic Prayer wherein the action of our Lord Jesus Christ at the _____ is re-enacted. The result, because of God's promise and presence, culminates in our participation in what is the most important and greatest sacrament and action of the Church. Why is this so? _____

19. What is the customary manner in which to receive the Holy Communion?

(**NOTE:** Some parishes practice intinction. This means the wafer is retained by the communicant and then dipped, by the priest or communicant, into the wine before placing it on the tongue. Also, the bishop may approve other ways in which to receive the bread and wine simultaneously.)

20. The *Book of Common Prayer* provides grounds for three specific reasons why a priest may refuse to allow a person to receive the Holy Communion, provided, however, that the priest notifies the bishop within fourteen days, giving the reasons for his or her actions. Where is this information found? _____

21. When persons for just cause and/or for extended periods of time are not able to be present at public celebrations of the Holy Eucharist, what special provision is made for them (see B.C.P., p. 396)? _____

In addition to this form providing for a shortened version of Rite One or Rite Two, a service is provided therein for communion to be given from what (see B.C.P.,

p. 396)? _____

22. At times and on occasions other than principal Sunday or weekday celebrations of the Holy Eucharist, such as house-Eucharists, retreat gatherings, etc., another form for celebrating the Holy Eucharist is provided. What is this called (see B.C.P.,

p. 400)? _____
What eight essential actions, after due preparation, must take place under these circumstances (see B.C.P., pp. 400-01)?

a. _____

b. _____

c. _____

d. _____ g. _____

e. _____ h. _____

f. _____

23. Where are the four accounts of the institution of the Holy Eucharist to be found in the Bible?

a. _____ c. _____

b. _____ d. _____

24. In many Christian denominations we often hear of people personally "accepting Jesus Christ as their Lord and Savior," and then of professing this commitment by walking forward to proclaim their faith, in what is commonly referred to

as an _____. It is important for Episcopalians to realize that we personally accept and receive Jesus Christ as our Lord and Savior at the

time of our _____ (our godparents speaking for us if we are children); we then personally confirm and ratify this acceptance of Jesus Christ

as our Lord and Savior at the time of our _____; and then

each time as we walk forward to God's altar for Holy Communion, we _____ our commitment to Jesus Christ as our Lord and Savior as we receive his

_____ into our life.

# Appendix:
# The Complete Prayer Book Subject and Topic Index

This index is divided into the following six categories:

General Information

Prayers

Thanksgivings

Canticles

Bible Passages

The Psalms: A Topic Index

The number following each entry denotes the page where this is to be found in the *Book of Common Prayer.* Where a prayer is not labeled as to subject and one or more such prayers occur on the same page, parentheses following the page number indicate the position of the particular prayer on that page. For example, 178(2) denotes the second prayer on page 178. The subject index of the Psalms, however, gives the number of the psalm and not the page number.

## General Information

Adoption of a child, directions for   439
Anointing, directions for   455
Articles of Religion   867
Ashes, blessing of   265
Ash Wednesday   264
Athanasius, Creed of St.   864

Banns of Marriage   437
Baptism, Holy   299
Baptism, directions for Holy   298; 312
Baptism, questions before   302
Baptismal Covenant   304; 416
Bishop, ordination of a   512
Bishop-Elect, examination of a   517
Blessing of a civil marriage   433
Burial of the Dead: Rite One   469
Burial of the Dead: Rite Two   491
Burial, An Order for   506
Burial, directions for   468; 490; 506; 507

Calendar of the Church Year   15
Calendar of Holy Days and Common of
   Saints   19
Canticles suggested at Evening Prayer   145
Canticles suggested at Morning Prayer   144
Catechism, The   845
Charitable bequests, on leaving   445
Chicago-Lambeth Quadrilateral   876
Chrism, Consecration of the   307
Christian Hope (Catechism)   861

Church (Catechism)   854
Collects (Common of Saints, Contemporary)
   246
Collects (Holy Days, Contemporary)   237
Collects (Seasons of the Year, Contemporary)
   211
Collects (Various Occasions, Contemporary)
   251
Collects (Common of Saints, Traditional)   195
Collects (Holy Days, Traditional)   185
Collects (Seasons of the Year, Traditional)   159
Collects (Various Occasions, Traditional)   199
Communion, exhortation before   316
Communion of the sick, directions for   396; 457
Communion under Special Circumstances   396
Compline   127
Concerning the Service of the Church   13
Conditional baptism, directions for   313
Confirmation   413
Confirmation, bishop's form for administering
   309; 418
Confirmation, directions for   412
Council of Chalcedon   864
Creeds (Catechism)   851

Daily Devotions for Individuals and Families
   136
Daily Evening Prayer: Rite One   61
Daily Evening Prayer: Rite Two   115
Daily Morning Prayer: Rite One   37

Daily Morning Prayer: Rite Two 75
Daily Office Lectionary, directions 934
Daily Office Lectionary (Holy Days) 996
Daily Office Lectionary (Seasons of the Year) 936
Daily Office Lectionary (Special Occasions) 1000
Daily Offices, directions for 36; 74; 141
Days of Optional Observance 17
Days of Special Devotion 17
Deacon, examination of a 543
Deacon, ordination of a 537
Decalogue, The 317; 350
Dedication and Consecration of a Church 567
Dedication and consecration of a church, directions for 566; 575
Disciplinary Rubrics 409

Emergency baptism, directions for 313
Eucharistic Lectionary A 889
Eucharistic Lectionary B 900
Eucharistic Lectionary C 911
Eucharistic Lectionary (Holy Days) 921
Eucharistic Lectionary (Common of Saints) 925
Eucharistic Lectionary (Various Occasions) 927
Exhortation, an 316
Exsultet 286

God the Father (Catechism) 846
God the Son (Catechism) 849
God the Holy Spirit (Catechism) 852
Good Friday 276
Great Vigil of Easter 285
Great Vigil of Easter, directions for 284

Historical Documents of the Church 864
Holy Days 16
Holy Baptism (See Baptism)
Holy Eucharist, An Order for Celebrating 400
Holy Eucharist: Rite One 323
Holy Eucharist: Rite Two 355
Holy Eucharist, directions for celebrating the 322; 354; 406
Holy Scriptures (Catechism) 853
Human Nature (Catechism) 845

Laying on of hands, directions for 455
Letter of Institution of a Minister 557
Litany, The Great 148
Litany for Ordinations 548
Litany for the nation 838
Litany of Thanksgiving 836

Marriage, Celebration and Blessing of a 423
Marriage, An Order for 435
Marriage, directions for 422; 433; 435
Maundy Thursday 274
Ministration to the Sick 453
Ministration at the Time of Death 462
Ministry (Catechism) 855

New Covenant (Catechism) 850
New Ministry, Celebration of a New 559
New ministry, directions for celebration of a 558; 564
Noonday prayer 103

Oath of allegiance for ordinations 513; 526; 538
Order of Worship for the Evening 108
Ordination rites, preface of 510
Ordination, general (See Deacon; Priest; or Bishop)
Outline of the Faith 845

Palm Sunday 270
Palms, blessing of 271
Penitential order (See Private Confession)
Prayer and Worship (Catechism) 856
Prayers and Thanksgivings 810
Prayers of the people, forms of 383
Preface of 1549 B.C.P. 866
Preface of 1789 B.C.P. 9
Priest, Ordination of a 525
Priest, examination of a 531
Principal Feasts 15
Private confession, directions for 446
Private confession, forms for 447; 449
Proper Liturgies for Special Days 263
Proper of Church Year, directions for 158
Proper Prefaces 344; 377
Psalter (Psalms of David) 585
Psalter, directions for 582

Ratification of 1789 B.C.P. 8
Reaffirmation, bishop's form for administering 310; 419
Reception, bishop's form for administering 310; 418
Reconciliation of a Penitent 447

Sacrament, when sickness prevents receiving 457
Sacramental Rites, Other (Catechism) 860
Sacraments (Catechism) 857
Sin and Redemption (Catechism) 848
Sundays 16

Table of Contents   5
Table of suggested canticles   144
Table to Find Movable Feasts and Holy Days
    884
Tables and Rules for Finding the Date of Easter
    880
Ten Commandments (Catechism)   847
Thanksgiving for birth or adoption   439
Titles of seasons, Sundays, and holy days   31

# Prayers

Absent, for the   830
Addiction, for victims of   831
Aged, for the   830
Agriculture, for   824
All Saints' Day   194; 245
All sorts and conditions of men, for   814
Alone, for those who live   829
Andrew, St.   185; 237
Anniversary of the Dedication of a Church,
    on the   204; 254
Annunciation, The   188; 240
Anointing with oil, at the   456(3, 4 and 5)
Answering of prayer, for the   834
Anxiety, in times of   165(1); 216(4)
Armed forces, for those in   823

Baptism, at   203; 254
Baptismal Covenant, for keeping the   163(1);
    214(3)
Baptized, for newly   310(3)
Baptized, for those about to be   305; 306; 819
Barnabas, St.   189; 241
Bartholomew, St.   192; 243
Bereavement, for a person in   831
Birthday, for a   830
Bishop, for a newly consecrated   521; 523
Body and soul, for health of   460

Charity, for   110(2); 164(4)
Child, for a sick   458; 459
Child, for the safe delivery of a   444
Child not yet baptized, for a   444
Children, for care of   829
Christ, for an increased knowledge of   173(3);
    225(2)
Christ, for those who do not know   280(1)
Christ's compassion, for   282
Christ's example, for following   180(4); 232(3);
    272(1 and 2)
Christ's life, for sharing in   162(2); 214(1)
Christ's presence, for abiding in   171(2); 223(1)
Christ's presence, for faith to perceive   174(2);
    226(1)

Christ's voice, for recognizing   173(2); 225(1)
Christ's work, for insight into   173(1); 224(4)
Christians, for all baptized   201; 252
Christmas prayer, a   160(3); 161(1 and 2);
    212(3 and 4); 213(1)
Chrysostom, Prayer of St.   59; 102; 126
Church, for the   280(3); 291(3); 515; 528; 540;
    816
Church family, for the   169(3); 221(2)
Church growth, for   289(2)
Church renewal, for   180(2); 232(1)
Cities, for   825
Clergy and people, for   817
Colleges, for   209; 261; 824
Commandments, for grace in keeping the
    164(3); 216(2)
Commerce and industry, for   208; 259
Communion, after receiving   834
Communion, before receiving   834
Confessions, private   447; 449
Confessions, general   41; 62; 79; 116; 127;
    267; 331; 352; 360; 397; 454
Confidence, for quiet   832
Confirmation, at   203; 254
Confirmed, for newly   418(1); 419(2)
Confirmed, for those about to be   305; 306(1)
Conflict, in times of   824
Congress, for   821
Conscience, for those who suffer for sake of
    823
Conservation of natural resources, for   827
Convention or meeting, for church   204; 255;
    818
Correctional institutions, for   826
Country, for our   820
Courts of justice, for   821
Crisis, in times of   180(1); 231(3)

Daily death to sin, for a   170(2); 222(1); 295(1)
Daily living, for grace in   182(3); 234(2)
Daily work, for vocation in   210; 261
Day, at the close of the   140
Death, a commendatory prayer at   465
Death, Commendation at the Time of   464;
    482; 499
Death, for a person near   462
Death, Litany at the Time of   462
Dedication of a church, at the   567; 568
    (1 and 2); 569(1)
Departed, committal of   484; 501
Departed, for the   202(1 and 2); 253; 464(2);
    470(1); 488(2 and 3); 493(1-3); 498(1 and 2);
    504(4)
Departed, intercession for the   480-81; 497-98

Departed child, for a   470(2); 494(1)
Diocese for the   817
Divine life of Christ, for sharing in the   288
Divine providence, for   177(3); 229(1)
Doctors and nurses, for   460

Easter Vigil, preparation during the   170(1 and 3); 221(3); 222(2); 283; 286-87; 295(2)
Education, for   209; 261
Election, for an   822
Election of a bishop or minister, for   818
Enemies, for our   816
Eternal life, for being kept in   294
Eternal truths, for perception of   182(2); 234(1)
Eucharistic prayers   333; 340; 361; 367; 369; 372; 402; 404; 408
Evangelical outreach, for   163(2 and 3); 215(1 and 2)
Evening, in early   139
Evening, in the   113(1 and 2); 133(1-4); 134(2 and 3); 833

Faith, hope, and charity, for the increase of   183(3); 235(2)
Faithful service, for   184(1); 235(3)
Families, for   828
Family blessing, a   441
Followers of Christ, for the   276
Francis, a prayer of St.   833
Fridays, for   56; 69; 99; 123
Funeral, prayer for vigil before a   465

God's Creation, for joy in   814
God's Creation, for knowledge of   827
God's gifts, for right use of   827
God's power, for   160(1); 212(1)
God's protection, for   167(1); 218(3)
God's will, for accomplishment of   430(2)
Government, for local   822
Government, for sound   821
Grace, for   57; 100; 183(1); 234(4)
Grace at meals   835
Grave, for consecration of a   487; 503
Guidance, for   57; 100; 179(2); 231(1); 832

Harmony with God and man, for   179(1); 230(4)
Harvest of lands and waters, for   828
Hastening of God's kingdom, for the   395(3)
Healing, for trust in God's   461
Health of body and soul, for   460
Heaven, for the attainment of   159(1); 162(3); 174(3); 211(1); 214(2); 226(2); 290(1); 505(1)
Holy Angels, of the   200; 251

Holy Communion, preparation before   167(2); 169(2); 171(1 and 3); 219(1); 221(1); 222(4); 223(2); 274; 397(3)
Holy Cross, of the   201; 252
Holy Cross Day   192; 244
Holy Eucharist, of the   201; 252
Holy Innocents, The   186; 238
Holy Spirit, for comfort of the   175(1); 226(3)
Holy Spirit, for direction of the   107(1)
Holy Spirit, for guidance of the   182(1); 233(3)
Holy Spirit, of the   200; 251
Holy Trinity, of the   199; 251
Human family, for the   815
Human race, for future of   828

Illness, for the sanctification of   460
Incarnation, of the   200; 252
Independence Day   190; 242
Inheritance of Israel, for rejoicing in the   289(3)
Inner peace, for   164(1); 215(3)
Intercession, general   57(4); 58(1 and 2); 70(4); 71(1 and 2); 100(3 and 4); 101(1); 124(3 and 4); 125(1); 277-79

James, St.   191; 242
James of Jerusalem, St.   193; 245
John, St.   186; 238
John the Baptist, Nativity of St.   190; 241
Joseph, St.   188; 239

Labor Day, for   210; 261
Leisure, for good use of   825
Life, for a proper respect for   489(1); 504(1)
Light of Christ, for the   161(3); 213(2)
Litany, The Great   148
Litany for Ordinations   548
Love, for the gift of   216(3)
Love, for those we   831
Love of Christ, for the   162(1); 213(3)
Love of God, for the   174(1); 181(2); 225(3); 233(1)
Luke, St.   193; 244

Malice and wickedness, for deliverance from   172(2); 224(1)
Mark, St.   188; 240
Married, for those about to be   425
Married, for those newly   429(1-7); 430(3); 431(1)
Married persons at a wedding, for all   430(1)
Martyr, of a   195; 246
Mary Magdalene   191; 242
Mary the Virgin, St.   192; 243
Matthew, St.   192; 244

Matthias, St.  188; 239
Members of the Church, for all  278(1)
Mercy and compassion, for  182(4); 234(3)
Michael and all Angels, St.  193; 244
Minister, for a new  560
Ministry, for choice of fit persons for  205; 256
Ministry, for effective  178(2); 230(1)
Mission, for power in  181(1); 232(4)
Mission of the Church, for  183(2); 206; 235(1); 257; 816
Missionary, for  196; 247
Monastic, of a  198; 249
Monastic orders and vocations, for  819
Morning, in the  137
Mourn, for those who  467(1); 489(4); 494(2); 505(2 and 3)
Musicians and artists, for church  819

Nation, for the  207; 258
Nations, for peace among  816
Need, in times of  179(3); 231(2)
Neglected, for the  826
Noonday, prayers at  107(1-4); 138(1 and 2)

Operation, before an  459
Oppressed, for the  826
Ordained, for those to be  205; 256
Ordinations, Litany for  548

Pain, in  461
Parents, for  444
Parish, for the  817
Paschal candle, at lighting of  285
Passion, in meditating on the  270
Pastor, of a  196; 248
Patience and humility of Christ, for the  168(1); 219(3)
Paul, Conversion of St.  187; 238
Peace, for  57; 69; 99; 123; 207; 258; 395(2); 815; 816
Perils, for aid against  70; 123; 177(1); 228(3)
Perplexity, in times of  178(1); 229(3)
Peter, Confession of St.  187; 238
Peter and Paul, Sts  190; 241
Philip and James, Sts  189; 240
Poor and neglected, for  826
Prayer, for the answering of  834
Prayers, for acceptance of our  394(1-4); 395(1)
Prayers of the People  328; 383; 385; 387; 388; 389; 392
Presence of Christ, for the  70; 124
Presentation, The  187; 239
President and civil authority, for  820
Priestly service, for effective  562

Prisons, for  826
Prophets, for grace to hear the  159(2); 211(2)
Protection, for  70; 124; 832
Public opinion, for those who influence  827
Purity of living, for  184(2); 236(1)

Quiet confidence, for  832

Rain, for  828
Reaffirmation, for those having made  419(2); 421
Reception of body at church, prayers for  466
Reign of Christ, of the  202; 254
Renewal of life, for  56; 99
Respecting God, for  178(3); 230(2)
Rest in Jesus, for those who  486
Resurrection, for faith in  504(3)
Righteous living, for  180(3); 232(2)
Rural areas, for  825

Saint, of a  198; 250
Saints, for the support of the  395(4)
Sanctification of illness, for the  460
Saturdays, for  56; 69; 99; 123
Schools and colleges, for  824
Scriptures, in studying the  184(3); 236(2)
Seasons, for fruitful  207; 258
Self-dedication, a prayer of  832
Self-purification, for  160(2); 212(2)
Shame and loss, in times of  168(3); 220(2)
Sick, for the  208; 260
Sick child, for a  458; 459
Sick person, for a  458; 461
Sickness, for recovery from  458
Simon and Jude, Sts  194; 245
Sin, for freedom from  164(2); 216(1)
Sin, for those fallen into  166(3); 218(2)
Sinful humanity, for  185(1); 236(3)
Sleep, for  461
Social justice, for  209; 260; 823
Social service, for  209; 260
Sorrow, for those who  467(1); 505(2 and 3)
Stability in Christ, for  167(3); 219(2)
State legislature, for  821
Stephen, St.  186; 237
Stewardship of Creation, for  208; 259
Strength and confidence in sickness, for  459
Strength in bearing our cross, for  165(2); 217(1)
Suffering, in times of  168(2); 169(1); 220(1); 220(3); 279
Sundays, for  56; 69; 98; 123; 170(4); 222(3); 835
Supplication, The  154

Temptation, in times of  166(2); 218(1)
Thankful living, for  289(1)

Thanksgiving Day 194; 246
Theologian and teacher, of a 197; 248
Thomas, St. 185; 237
Towns and rural areas, for 825
Transfiguration, The 191; 243
Transformation of character, for 166(1); 217(2); 264
Travelers, for 831
Trinity, in glorification of the 176(1); 228(1)
Trouble, for a person in 155; 831
Trust in God, for 181(3); 233(2)

Unemployed, for the 824
Unity of the Church, for 178(4); 204; 230(3); 255; 818

Vigil prayers before a funeral 465
Visitation, The 189; 240
Vocation, for all Christians in their 206; 256

Water of life, for the 290(2)
Whitsunday, on 175; 227
World leaders, for 278(2)
World order, for 177(2); 229(1)
Worship, after 153; 834
Worship, before 833
Worthiness in our calling, for 176(2); 228(2)

Young persons, for 829

# Thanksgivings

Beauty of the earth, for 840
Beginning of recovery from illness, for 460

Communion, for 339; 365; 366; 399; 457
Communion at burial, for 482; 498
Communion at marriage, for 432
Communion at ordination of bishop, for 523
Communion at ordination of deacon, for 546
Communion at ordination of priest, for 535

Deliverance from sin, for 172(3); 224(2)
Diversity of races and cultures, for 840

General Thanksgiving 58(3); 71(3); 101(2); 125(2); 836
Gift of a child, for 841

Harvest, for the 840
Heroic service, for 488(4); 839

Litany of Thanksgiving 837
Litany of Thanksgiving for a Church 578

Mission of the Church, for 838

Nation, for the 838
Newly baptized, by 311(2)
Newly baptized, for 308(1); 309(1); 314

Over water at baptism 306

Renewal of baptismal vows, for 292
Restoration of health, for 841

Saints and faithful departed, for 487(2); 488(1); 489(2); 503(3); 504(2); 838

Thanksgiving at birth or adoption 441-43

Waters of baptism, for 569(2); 570

# Canticles

Christ our Passover, *Pascha nostrum* 46; 83

First Song of Isaiah, *Ecce, Deus* 86

Glory be to God, *Gloria in excelsis* 52
Glory to God, *Gloria in excelsis* 94

Jubilate, *Psalm 100* 45; 82

O Gracious Light, *Phos hilaron* 64; 112; 118; 139

Second Song of Isaiah, *Quarerite Dominum* 86
Song of Creation, *Benedicite, omnia opera Domini* 47; 88
Song of Mary, *Magnificat* 50; 65; 91; 119
Song of Moses, *Cantemus Domino* 85
Song of Penitence *Kyrie Pantokrator* 90
Song of Praise, *Benedictus es, Domine* 49; 90
Song of Simeon, *Nunc dimittis* 51; 66; 93; 120; 140
Song of the Redeemed, *Magna et mirabilia* 94
Song of Zechariah, *Benedictus Dominus Deus* 50; 92
Song to the Lamb, *Dignus es* 93

Third Song of Isaiah, *Surge, illuminare* 87

Venite, *Ps. 95:1-7* 44; 82; 146

We Praise Thee, *Te Deum laudamus* 52

You Are God, *Te Deum laudamus* 95

# Bible Passages

Acts 1:8   39; 77
Amos 5:8   62; 115

1 Chron. 29:11   344; 377
Col. 1:12   40; 77
Col. 3:1   39; 77
1 Cor. 5:7-8   46; 83
1 Cor. 15:20-22   46; 83
2 Cor. 13:14   59; 72; 102; 126

Dan. 9:9-10   38; 76

Eph. 2:19   40; 78
Eph. 3:20-21   60; 73; 102; 126
Eph. 5:2   343; 376
Exod. 15:1-6, 11-13, 17-18   85

Hab. 2:20   40; 78
Heb. 4:14, 16   320; 352
Heb. 9:24   39; 77
Heb. 13:15-16   344; 376
Heb. 13:20-21   132

Isa. 12:2-6   86
Isa. 26:3; 30:15   138
Isa. 40:3   37; 75
Isa. 40:5   37; 75
Isa. 49:6b   38; 76
Isa. 53:6   39; 76
Isa. 55:6-11   86
Isa. 57:15   40; 78
Isa. 60:1-3, 11a, 14c, 18-19   87
Isa. 60:3   38; 76

Jer. 14:9, 22   131; 140
Joel 2:13   38; 76
John 3:16   332; 396; 449
John 4:23   40; 78
John 6:35   396
John 6:51, 55-56   397
John 8:12   62; 116
John 15:4-5a, 8-9   397
1 John 1:8-9   38; 76; 320; 352
1 John 2:1-2   332; 450

Lam. 1:12   39; 77
Luke 1:46-55   50; 65; 91; 119; 441
Luke 1:68-79   50; 92
Luke 2:10-11   37; 75
Luke 2:29-32   51; 66; 93; 120
Luke 15:18-19   38; 76

Mal. 1:11   38; 76; 106
Mark 8:34   38; 76
Mark 12:29-31   351
Mark 13:35-36   37; 75
Matt. 5:14-16   109
Matt. 5:23-24   343; 376
Matt. 11:28   332; 449
Matt. 22:37-40   319

1 Pet. 1:3   137
1 Pet. 5:8-9a   132
Phil. 1:2   40; 61; 78; 115
Pr. of Man. 1-2, 4, 6-7, 11-15   90
Ps. 4   128
Ps. 16:7-8   60; 115
Ps. 19:4   40; 78
Ps. 19:14   40; 78
Ps. 23   443; 476
Ps. 27   477
Ps. 31   129
Ps. 42   471
Ps. 43:3   40; 78
Ps. 46   471
Ps. 50:14   343; 376
Ps. 51   137; 266
Ps. 74:15-16   61; 115
Ps. 90   472
Ps. 91   129
Ps. 95:1-7   44; 82
Ps. 95   146
Ps. 96:8   343; 376
Ps. 96:9   61; 115
Ps. 96:9, 13   44
Ps. 100   45, 82
Ps. 105:1   40; 78
Ps. 106   478
Ps. 113   138
Ps. 116   442; 478
Ps. 118:24   39; 77
Ps. 119   103
Ps. 121   104; 473
Ps. 122:1   40; 78
Ps. 126   105
Ps. 130   474
Ps. 134   131; 140
Ps. 139:10-11   62; 110; 116
Ps. 139   474
Ps. 141:2   61; 115

Rev. 4:8   39; 77
Rev. 4:11   93; 344; 377
Rev. 5:9-10, 13   93
Rev. 15:3-4   94

Rev. 21:3  37; 75
Rom. 6:9-11  46; 83
Rom. 12:1  343; 376
Rom. 15:13  60; 73; 102; 126

Song of Three Young Men 35-65  47; 88
Song of Three Young Men 29-34  49; 90

1 Tim. 1:15  332; 449

# The Psalms: A Topic Index

*NOTE: The listing below is by psalm number.*

Church, the  46; 48; 84; 111; 122; 133; 147

Divine guidance  25; 43; 80; 85; 111; 112

Evening  4; 13; 16; 17; 31:1-6; 77; 91; 121; 134

God our refuge  4; 17; 20; 37; 46; 49; 54; 61; 71; 91; 103; 121; 146
God the Creator  8; 19; 33; 65; 104; 111; 145; 147
God the Judge  1; 7; 11; 46; 50; 62; 75; 76; 82; 90; 96; 97; 98
God the Redeemer  33; 102:15; 103; 111; 113; 114; 126; 130; 138
God's glory  18:1-20; 29; 36:5; 46; 99; 148; 150
God's law  19; 50; 62; 111; 119; 147
God's mercy  23; 32; 57; 61; 62; 63; 73; 77; 85; 86; 100; 103; 118; 130; 145
God's providence  23; 33; 34; 37:26; 89:1-19; 121; 124; 139; 145; 146; 147
God's sovereignty  24; 46; 47; 72; 89:1-19; 93; 96; 97; 98; 99; 112; 145; 146
God's wisdom  33; 104; 111; 113; 139; 145; 147

Hope of immortality  16; 30; 42; 49; 66; 73; 103; 116; 121; 139; 146

Incarnation, the  2; 8; 85; 89:1-30; 102:15; 110; 111; 113; 132

Morning  3; 5; 20; 63; 90; 143

Passion, the  22; 40:1-16; 42; 54; 69:1-22, 30-37; 88; 116; 130
Peace  29; 46; 76; 85; 98; 100; 124; 125; 126
Penitence  6; 32; 38; 51; 102; 130; 143
Prayer  4; 5; 17; 20; 28; 31; 54; 61; 84; 86; 102:15; 141:1-4; 142
Preparation for Holy Communion  23; 25; 26; 36:5; 41; 43; 63; 84; 85; 86; 122; 130; 133; 139

Righteousness  1; 11; 12; 15; 18:21-35; 19; 26; 34; 40:1-16; 92; 111; 112

Thanksgiving  30; 65; 67; 92; 98; 100; 103; 107; 111; 116; 134; 138; 145; 147; 148; 150
Thanksgiving after Holy Communion  8; 15; 18:1-20; 19; 27; 29; 30; 34; 100; 103; 110; 118; 145; 150
Transitoriness of life  39; 40; 90; 102:15
Trouble, in time of  3; 11; 12; 13; 18:1-20; 20; 30; 40:1-16; 46; 49; 57; 62; 63; 80; 85; 86; 90; 107:1-16; 118; 144; 146
Trust in God  27; 31; 57; 62; 63; 71; 73; 77; 91; 118; 121; 123; 124; 125; 143; 146

Worship  5; 26; 43; 63; 65; 66; 67; 84; 96; 100; 102:15; 116; 122; 138

83947